100 Unique
Eats and Eateries
in Missouri

Ann M. Hazelwood

REEDY PRESS
St. Louis, Missouri

Reedy Press
PO Box 5131
St. Louis, MO 63139
USA

Library of Congress Control Number: 2009920387

ISBN: 978-1-933370-84-2

Please visit our website at www.reedypress.com.

Printed in the United States of America
09 10 11 12 13   5 4 3 2 1

All images in the book were provided by the respective restaurants. Thank you to those restaurants who shared their photography.

design by Bruce Burton

Contents

DEDICATION

To my husband, Keith Hazelwood, who continues to share many restaurant experiences with me, thank you for your love and patience. To my talented sons, Joel and Jason Watkins, I will always be grateful for your love and support.

MISSOURI'S BEST

Missouri's travel is at its best when we look for food to test.

Ethnic flavors can here be found, as ancestors settled on our ground.

The roadside diners that we can smell create "the meal" for which we tell.

The barbeque of this dear state is smoked and pulled to make it great.

Along the river, give us wine, its aroma and bite are really fine.

Show me Missouri, when it's time to eat, then add some fun to make complete!

Foreword

As Lieutenant Governor of the State of Missouri, I have met wonderful people in every corner of our state. From the rolling hills of the Ozarks to the metropolitan blocks of our great cities, Missouri's heritage and culture is rich and diverse. During my travels, I have encountered some of the best restaurants, diners and cafés that our state has to offer. From traditional Kansas City barbeque to the birthplace of cashew chicken in Springfield to the marvelous Italian cuisine of The Hill in St. Louis, our state has many unique eateries that tell the story of our people.

In her newest book, Ann Hazelwood takes us on a journey across the Show-Me State into the most unique eateries you will ever find. It is my hope that you will use this book as a food lover's guide to Missouri.

Please enjoy this book and dive into Missouri's rich and varied culinary traditions.

PETER D. KINDER

Lieutenant Governor of the State of Missouri

Introduction

Missouri is so good at so many things, and our food and restaurants are at the top of the list. What we excel at helps define who we are, and a signature dish at a unique eatery hints at the state's heritage, passion, and diversity.

Restaurants and specialty foods abound in Missouri. We not only love eating ballpark hot dogs while taking in a game, but we also occasionally want to be a part of the action—by catching a "throwed roll" or two. We will pit our barbeque against any state in the nation. And whether we are licking barbeque sauce, melted provel cheese, or gooey butter from our fingers, the "food experience" is an important part of our daily lives. Also, special occasions and vacations are often rated by our dining experiences.

The eateries compiled in this volume display the diversity and unique quality of restaurant dining in Missouri. These one hundred establishments have elevated Missouri's restaurant bar, and they offer visitors unforgettable experiences not only with the culinary arts but also with superb service, attention to detail, and ambience.

Everyone wants food at its very best, so it is helpful to know an eatery's signature item. Many menus offer a number of strong dishes, but sometimes it helps to know when to save room for dessert or when a certain appetizer is absolutely necessary. For each restaurant, I make one recommendation that would truly help you savor your dining experience.

My food adventure through the Show Me State not only serves up the dishes that make Missouri food unique, but it goes far beyond the food as well. Ambience is essential. Dine in a museum, on a bluff, in cave, or in a historic building. Learn the backstory of the restaurant—some are generational, some are groundbreaking, and some are haunted!

My sincere appreciation to the many Missourians throughout the state who generously offered their suggestions for this book. And kudos to the wonderful chefs and restaurateurs who work hard to give us that great food experience. Also, many thanks to my favorite travel companion and loving husband, Keith Hazelwood, who shares my love of good food and unique places.

Travel light, bring this book, and bon appetit!

ANN M. HAZELWOOD

Hamburger Fun!

Everyone loves a good hamburger, but no one likes a hamburger that ends up on your lap. Janet and Matt Bass created KRUMBLY BURGER, a fun hamburger eatery in Troy. And the trick is keeping all the burger bits off your lap and in your mouth.

The Bass secret blend is basically a sauceless Sloppy Joe, which is loosely crumbled on the bun. You can order these delights in small, medium, and large. A variety of condiments are offered, but the barbeque sauce, mustard, pickles, and onions are the favorites. Some claim this "steam burger" is healthier than its standard counterpart, since all the grease is drained away.

This bargain burger leaves room in your budget to order some tasty onion straws. These popular skinny fried onions are a meal unto themselves, so you may want to share. It is a perfect combo in a diner-like atmosphere. Can you eat the burger without it crumbling?

WHAT ELSE IS ON THE MENU? Strawberry Cheesecake in a Cup

WHAT'S NEARBY? Located in the heart of the Troy business district

HOW DO I GET THERE? 70 Front St.; Off Hwy. 47 to Front St.

HOW TO CONTACT 636-528-5646

From Dairy Queen to Filets

Who could have imagined that the shell of a one-time favorite Dairy Queen in St. Charles would house a cozy, gourmet boutique restaurant called PREMIERE CAFE? Jim Thomas and Damon Barber started with a catering business in 1996, and in 2002 they spotted the vacant Dairy Queen, right in the heart of the Frenchtown Historic District.

Filets are the meal of choice among frequent customers. The prime cuts are prepared with Premiere's own seasoning and garnished with their Maitre D' butter, which melts in your mouth. A trio of amaretto carrots, green beans, and roasted potatoes complement this dinner selection.

Seasonal seating is available on the building's side patio. If you prefer to eat inside, get your reservation in early for this thirty-seat, white-tablecloth restaurant.

WHAT ELSE IS ON THE MENU? Roasted Chicken Parmesan

WHAT'S NEARBY? Historic Frenchtown

HOW DO I GET THERE? 1116 N. 2nd St.; I-70 to 5th St., to Clark, then left to 2nd St.

HOW TO CONTACT 636-940-9500

3

Branson's Best

For one of the best dining experiences when you visit the No. 1 tourist destination in Missouri, try the CANDLESTICK INN in Branson. This award-winning restaurant has the most awesome view overlooking Lake Taneycomo, according to the *Springfield News-Leader*. This romantic spot beckons you to try one of the one hundred martinis or one of the many upscale wines on the menu.

The first course should be the delicious Candlestick shrimp dish, Chandelier Crevette (French for "shrimp," of course). The shrimp is hickory smoked and then wrapped in apple-smoked bacon, and it is served with a zippy ground mustard sauce. Next, try a Capri Salad, followed by the South African lobster. Delightful homemade desserts cap the evening, if you dare!

Jim and Brandon Cox, owners since 1997, are carrying on the high standards of the Campells, who started the restaurant in 1962.

WHAT ELSE IS ON THE MENU? Lobster Bisque

WHAT'S NEARBY? Branson's Landing and downtown Branson

HOW DO I GET THERE? 127 Taney St.; Hwy. 65, East Hwy. 76, Candlestick Rd. to Taney St.

HOW TO CONTACT 417-334-3633 | www.candlestickinn.com

Spam on What?

Jeff Newton and Brad Steenhoek in Kirksville named their bistro IL SPAZIO (Italian for "space") because of the spaciousness of the building, which once housed an automobile dealership.

What truly has become a community center is known for its wood-fired oven pizza and its Shepherd's Pie. The Shepherd's Pie has coffee-marinated ground chuck, mixed with spices and Boulevard Stout beer from Kansas City. The adventuresome diner might try one of their unusual and popular pizzas, like the Spam and Doritos special. Yes, Spam!

Il Spazio's unique and tasty food and large variety of martinis, wines, and beers make it an indispensable stop in this college town. The eclectic and fun atmosphere are a bonus!

WHAT ELSE IS ON THE MENU? Mediterranean Steaks and Seafood

WHAT'S NEARBY? One block from County Court House Square

HOW DO I GET THERE? 215 W. Washington; I-63 to E. Washington

HOW TO CONTACT 660-665-8484 | www.ilspazio.com

More Than a Cup of Coffee

If you are in downtown West Plains or visiting the campus of Missouri State University, you will want to get more than a cup of coffee at CUP O' JOE CAFÉ. Owner Joann Williams Nelson chose clever-named sandwiches and salads that are all big sellers. The Black Sheep Sandwich—ham, turkey, roast beef, salami, and Swiss cheese on buttermilk sourdough bread—is a meal in itself. Each sandwich is then garnished with two different secret blends, Zing sauce and Romano cheese sauce. A panini grill blends the flavors, and the result leaves you in heaven.

The café encourages lounging, with a large-screen television, leather couches, and free WIFI. If you bring along the younger set, Cup O' Joe's offers a play area as well. This historic structure right off the town square appeals to students and businessmen alike.

WHAT ELSE IS ON THE MENU? Chicago-Style Pizza

WHAT'S NEARBY? Missouri State University, one block away

HOW DO I GET THERE? 111 N. Washington Ave.; I-44, to I-63, to Thayer/W. Plains I-63 S. to Court House Square to Washington

HOW TO CONTACT 417-256-0689 | www.cupojoecafe.com

6

Pork Chop Heaven

Nestled among the towns of Kirksville, Hannibal, and Moberly is tiny Bevier, home to some seven hundred residents and one hidden gem—the PEAR TREE RESTAURANT. The Pear Tree has been around for twenty-three years, and owner Al Abbadessa said its extensive menu attracts customers from far and wide.

The buzz is all about the pork chops. Each chop weighs in at one pound and is usually around one inch thick. Try them barbequed or plain, but almost everyone orders their chops with garlic mashed potatoes.

Two hundred and fifty people can be seated in this nondescript brick historic building, once home to a bank. Some claim it is haunted because of a well-known bank robbery that took place there years ago.

This award-winning eatery is well worth the trip!

WHAT ELSE IS ON THE MENU? Batter-Dipped Lobster Tail

WHAT'S NEARBY? 5 minutes from Macon

HOW DO I GET THERE? 222 N. Macon St.; I-36 to Hwy. C

HOW TO CONTACT 660-773-6666 | www.thepeartreerestaurant.com

Smokehouse Special

There is a lot that's special about PORKY'S SMOKE-HOUSE in Mexico, Missouri. The lunch crowd packs this multiroom café that displays beautiful mounted animals on all the walls. Country music interspersed with chatter from the dining crowd provides the ambience.

The Smoked Prime Rib is the hot menu item on Friday and Saturday nights. Hungry customers know they will be satisfied with this fourteen-ounce, inch-and-a-half-thick delight. Two sides and Texas toast accompany this generous entrée.

Porky's authentic pit barbeque has put Mexico on the map, and *Rural Missouri Magazine* listed it among its picks for best in the Midwest. You will know you are at the right place when you see "Porky the Pig" by the front door!

WHAT ELSE IS ON THE MENU? Large Fresh-Cut Seasoned French Fries

WHAT'S NEARBY? Downtown Mexico and Missouri Military Academy

HOW DO I GET THERE? 1100 E. Liberty St.; I-54 to East Liberty and Martin Luther King Dr.

HOW TO CONTACT 573-581-5442

A Whopper of a Pizza

Pizza doesn't get any bigger—or better—than the twenty-eight-inch pie at MONETTI'S PIZZE-RIA in Warrensburg. This monster weighs seven to eight pounds depending on your choice of toppings. The New York–style thin crust is freshly tossed, if you can imagine, and covered with only fresh ingredients. The "Gigunda Eating Challenge" rewards you with one hundred dollars if you and a partner can eat this pizza in one hour. Eight to ten people can eat heartily with one pizza. No doubt it is the biggest pizza in Johnson County!

Since 2004, the Monetti family has brought their Sicilian and Roman heritage to their cooking. You can watch many of the dishes being prepared in their open kitchen.

Patio dining is also available. Take your time, you'll need it!

WHAT ELSE IS ON THE MENU? Italian Sausage Calzone

WHAT'S NEARBY? 2 blocks from downtown Warrensburg

HOW DO I GET THERE? 214 E. Coulton; I-70, exit 49 toward Warrensburg, Mo. 13 to East Coulton

HOW TO CONTACT 660-747-8888 | www.monettis.com

Thanks for the Memories!

The BROADWAY DINER in Columbia ensures you will have the true experience of an old-fashioned diner, with all the fixings. Hubert Blakeman opened the establishment in 1949. Since 1963, it has been in the hands of Ed Johnson, who loves his history! Once located on Broadway, it was relocated to make room for a Walgreen's.

The Stretch is the diner's most notable menu item: a three-egg omelet, covered with diced green onions, green peppers, and shredded pepper jack cheese rest atop a bed of hash browns. You can top it off with chili or with ranch dressing loaded with Tabasco sauce and sliced jalapenos. The diner averages two hundred orders of their specialty daily—and that's no stretch!

WHAT ELSE IS ON THE MENU? Triple Berry Pancakes with Blueberries, Raspberries, and Strawberries

WHAT'S NEARBY? Historic Flat Branch Park and two blocks from Missouri University

HOW DO I GET THERE? 22 S. 4th St.; I-70 to Providence to 4th St.

HOW TO CONTACT 573-875-1173

Food and History All in One!

A great eatery stop and educational opportunity is right off of I-70. The little town of Williamsburg is fortunate to have MARLENE'S RESTAURANT AND CRANE'S MUSEUM, all in the same building.

You will want to bring your appetite when you walk through the door, because a scrumptious French Dip sandwich awaits you. The beef is grilled with onions that create an au jus for dipping. The meat is smothered with Swiss cheese and served on a hoagie bun. Extra juice is always available, and the tender beef can be purchased in their country store located next door. Typical sides include homemade slaw or potato salad.

If you stop in during the winter, Marlene makes her homemade chili, which is worth the seasonal wait!

Proprietors Joe and Marlene Crane offer their patrons a unique eating environment, to say the least. While indulging your appetite, take in a bit of history through their collection of Missouri artifacts.

WHAT ELSE IS ON THE MENU? Homemade Pies and
Blackberry Cobbler

WHAT'S NEARBY? The museum attached and
Crane's Country Store next door

HOW DO I GET THERE? 10665 Old Hwy. 40; ½ mile
off the I-70, Williamsburg exit

HOW TO CONTACT 877-254-3356 | www.cranesmuseum.org

A Classy Breakfast

You will love having breakfast in a classy café presented in nice black and white décor, or you can sit out on the sidewalk overlooking Country Club Plaza in Kansas City, Missouri. These choices are yours when you visit the CLASSIC CUP CAFÉ.

The menu is overwhelming, but a quick scan of customers reveals most are enjoying the Classic Eggs Benedict. The base of two English muffins is covered with basil spread to give it a little kick. Ham and poached eggs—covered with Hollandaise sauce—complete this mouth-watering breakfast. This signature menu item is served with a mound of cubed fries.

Four owners and renowned chefs known for their international cuisine are on hand to present this experience. Lunch and dinner also are available.

WHAT ELSE IS ON THE MENU? 10-inch Pancakes

WHAT'S NEARBY? Barnes and Noble is across the street, along with other upscale shops

HOW DO I GET THERE? 301 West 47th St.; I-70, I-35, to Country Club Plaza

HOW TO CONTACT 816-753-1840 | www.classiccup.com

A Buffet Like No Other

Move over Las Vegas. CHARLEY'S BUFFET in Lincoln can out cook, out sell, out talk, and out eat any buffet across the country. Charley Piecer and his extended Mennonite family cook and serve in this large 235-seat restaurant.

You will be greeted with an expansive selection that includes more than sixty desserts, at least four meat selections, and an endless army of side dishes.

Charley's Buffet plays hard-to-get when it comes to his hungry customers. Its location nine miles outside Cole Camp places it among nothing more than a few homes, but it's definitely worth the trip. Since Charley's is only open on Friday and Saturday nights from 4:30 p.m. to 8:30 p.m., you will see lines around this huge building waiting to get in, no matter the season.

The weekly preparation of this entirely homemade food extravaganza is worth waiting for.

WHAT ELSE IS ON THE MENU? Baked Sauerkraut with Brown Sugar and Hot Dogs

WHAT'S NEARBY? Six miles from the Lake of the Ozarks

HOW DO I GET THERE? Located at the corner of B and W; take I-65 to H to W

HOW TO CONTACT 660-668-3806

13

The Real Cheeseburger

There is no fast food at KEITH'S CAFÉ in Memphis, Missouri. This community, population two thousand, is spoiled by a sixty-year-old restaurant owned by Everett Keith and his son, Everett, Jr.

Cheeseburgers and more cheeseburgers are the main menu item. Once the steaks are cut and freshly ground each day, they are molded into patties and stacked for frying alongside thick slices of American cheese.

For the dinner crowd, you can count on steaks to be a big favorite. The T-bones weigh three pounds each.

During the month of January, the café closes for a good cleaning. Zelda, Everett's wife, washes hundreds of coffee cups that cover the ceiling. The walls display other collectibles and memorabilia. The last day before he closes and the first day he reopens, there is standing-room only!

WHAT ELSE IS ON THE MENU? Home-Cut French Fries

WHAT'S NEARBY? Six blocks from the town square of Memphis

HOW DO I GET THERE? 470 S. Market St.; just off Hwy. 136

HOW TO CONTACT 660-465-8581

14

It's All About Mexican in Mexico

When it is time for a special meal or snack after a movie, the residents of Mexico flock to EL VAQUERO for delicious Mexican food.

Following an early feast of chips and awesome salsa, patrons often order the popular Monterey Chicken. A very tender chicken breast is grilled and covered with queso dip, then served with lettuce, tomatoes, rice, and beans. The meal includes two side dishes.

Just to note, the menu is huge and lengthy, and the margaritas seem to be a standard companion of nearly every meal. The flavors are lime, strawberry, peach, and the house favorite, "Margarita on the Rocks."

WHAT ELSE IS ON THE MENU? Grapefruit-Size Fried Ice Cream Served in a Taco Shell with Whipped Cream and Chocolate Syrup

WHAT'S NEARBY? Lakeview Park

HOW DO I GET THERE? 2780 S. Clark; three miles from Bus. 54

HOW TO CONTACT 573-581-5730

John Deere to Family Restaurant

When you live in Albany, Missouri, you know most every location, because the town has only two thousand people. What used to be a John Deere implement store is now a young Mormon family's eatery called POPPA'S RESTAURANT. Kristy and Randy Poppa previously had a restaurant that specialized in Mexican food, so along with a popular American menu, they introduced Mexican food to Albany.

Chili Relleno is a chili pepper sliced and stuffed with cheese and pepper mixture, wrapped in homemade bread dough, frozen, and then deep-fried. It is served with enchilada sauce and cheese and comes with fiesta rice, salad, and a beef enchilada.

Four of the Poppa family's seven children help out in the restaurant. A large banquet room is being added. A small meeting room and an active children's room are very busy. It truly is a family restaurant!

WHAT ELSE IS ON THE MENU? Kristy's Special Peanut Butter Pie

WHAT'S NEARBY? Albany's Municipal Airport

HOW DO I GET THERE? 1204 W. Hwy. 136; I-70, I-435, I-35, Hwy. 13, toward Bethany to Hwy. 136

HOW TO CONTACT 660-726-5577

A Taste of Argentina

PIROPOS Briarcliff Restaurant in Kansas City, Missouri, will take you to Argentina not only with its unique, extensive menu but also with its décor. *Piropos* means "an enormous compliment" in Spanish. Its owners make sure you feel the same presence of the culture in their antiques, art murals, and glass, which are all imported from Spain.

Don't be surprised if they recommend their "melt in your mouth" eight-ounce Peppercorn Encrusted Filet served in a brandy cream sauce. It is accompanied by au gratin potatoes and tasty sautéed mushrooms.

Argentinean dining is very cosmopolitan, with a touch of Spanish, Italian, and French, creating a variety of flavor that is not spicy. The dining room's large windows offer an incredible view of Kansas City's skyline. The view at dusk is absolutely breathtaking as the lights begin to twinkle. For a romantic and pleasant dining experience, you will want to try this taste of Argentina.

WHAT ELSE IS ON THE MENU? Copa Piropos (ice cream with berries)

WHAT'S NEARBY? A charming shopping village with upscale shops

HOW DO I GET THERE? 4141 Mulberry Dr.; 5 miles north of Kansas City off Hwys. 71 and 169

HOW TO CONTACT 816-741-3600 | www.piroposkc.com

What's Wild at the Wild Onion?

In 2000, Pam Infranca opened a restaurant in Trenton, which she purchased from Lela Belle Brinster. Keeping a popular restaurant successful was her challenge. Pam renamed the restaurant WILD ONION FLOWERS AND CAFÉ and tweaked the menu to reflect what she thought the locals would enjoy.

She hit the jackpot when she introduced her Baked Pork Chops. Pam said she uses the best Iowa chops and makes her gravy with real buttermilk. Add her special mashed potatoes and fried apples and you have the best comfort food known to man!

With this home-cooked menu becoming such a success, she expanded her restaurant in 2005. You can dine at the counter, at tables of four, or in private booths. Friday night dining is by candlelight.

The Wild Onion also serves as a full-service florist.

WHAT ELSE IS ON THE MENU? Cherry Cobbler with Vanilla Bean Ice Cream

WHAT'S NEARBY? North Central Missouri College

HOW DO I GET THERE? 1115 Main St.; I-70, I-63, I-65, 9th, 12th to Main

HOW TO CONTACT 660-359-3050 | www.thewildonioncafe.com

The Charm of Pierce City

Pierce City is lucky to have not only a great restaurant called FREDA MAE'S TEA ROOM AND EATERY, but also its proprietor Lynnette Rector, who cares about the history of this small town. The town and restaurant were destroyed by a tornado in 2003. Lynnette salvaged what memorabilia she could from the remnants, creating a display that is among the highlights of the restaurant and its amazing gift shop.

All of Freda Mae's breads and desserts are made fresh daily. For lunch, try Freda Mae's Specialty: homemade bread, salami, ham, mozzarella cheese, lettuce, tomatoes, black olives, and Dijon mustard, all battered and butter grilled.

In summer, dine on the old-fashioned patio with a stone waterfall. The bakery and gift shop are clearly a result of Lynnette's excellent taste!

WHAT ELSE IS ON THE MENU? Open-Faced Roast Beef Dinner

WHAT'S NEARBY? Downtown Pierce City

HOW DO I GET THERE? 101 E. Commercial; I-44 eleven miles to I-97, then to Commercial

HOW TO CONTACT 417-476-5717 | www.fredamaes.com

An Elegant Starter

The Raphael Hotel in Kansas City is one of few historic boutique hotels in Missouri, and the only one that houses elegant RAPHAEL RESTAURANT, with its creative Continental cuisine.

After choosing one of the magnificent wines, you will want to try their famous Crab Cakes. Peter Hahn, the executive chef, understands first impressions. His Maryland-style backfin crab cakes are 100 percent crab meat, unlike most other cakes. The two generous cakes are placed on top of delicious scallion mashed potatoes. Spiced and roasted pepper sauce and corn relish are served on the side.

Many more entrée choices are available, all in one of their cozy rooms, creating an intimate dining experience. A small lounge adjoins the restaurant where you can enjoy an after-dinner drink and some fine piano music.

WHAT ELSE IS ON THE MENU? New Zealand Rack of Lamb with Truffle Risotto

WHAT'S NEARBY? Country Club Plaza, with upscale shopping and water canal

HOW DO I GET THERE? 325 Ward Pkwy.; Hwy. 71, Volker Blvd., to Ward Pkwy.

HOW TO CONTACT 816-756-3800 | www.raphaelkc.com

All About Chipotle Chicken

BEKS in Fulton includes its special Chipotle Marinated Chicken in various menu favorites. For lunch, it's the Chipotle Chicken Sandwich, grilled and topped with gruyere cheese and served with chipotle aioli. If you join the dinner rush, your chipotle option is Chicken Pasta, which has alfredo sauce with spicy jalapeños, onions, garlic, green peppers, and parmesan cheese and is served with a crispy salad and hot bread.

This historic three-story restaurant was once a dry goods store. Enjoy a special treat: turn-of-the-century photos of B. F. Oliver, displayed on the walls.

This rustic, elegant eatery is a must visit when in Fulton.

<u>WHAT ELSE IS ON THE MENU?</u> A Starbucks Coffee House in the same building

<u>WHAT'S NEARBY?</u> The Winston Churchill Museum

<u>HOW DO I GET THERE?</u> 511 Court St.; I-70, Hwy. 54 to Rt. F, which turns into 4th St.

<u>HOW TO CONTACT</u> 573-592-7117 | www.beksshop.com

Pig Out in a Dining Car!

Sedalia is known for more than hosting the Missouri State Fair. KEHDE'S BARBEQUE started as a Dog N' Suds in the 1950s and in 1993 moved to a location with an attached railroad dining car.

A wide variety of barbeque is on the menu, but if you order the "Miss Piggy" Sandwich, you won't be disappointed! Roger Kehde cooks for his father, John, who owns the restaurant. John deep fries the slice of tenderloin and places it on a Kaiser roll. Inside, a slice of provolone cheese, smoked ham, lettuce, tomatoes, and onion all are topped with John's special sauce of mayonnaise and Thousand Island dressing. Now we know how this sandwich got its name!

Kehde's offers a casual lunch and dinner environment for the whole family. Look for the green railroad car along the highway.

WHAT ELSE IS ON THE MENU? Fried Pickles and Onion Blooms

WHAT'S NEARBY? Sedalia State Fairgrounds across the street

HOW DO I GET THERE? 1915 S. Limit (Hwy. 65); I-70 to Exit 78A, merge to I-65 toward Sedalia

HOW TO CONTACT 660-826-2267

Lunch at Forest Park

Visiting the beautiful, historic Forest Park is indeed a treat in itself, but enjoying fine quality food amid the bucolic atmosphere is extra special. The BOATHOUSE RESTAURANT, operated by Catering St. Louis, is located on one of the park lakes. Before or after your meal, enjoy a boat ride through the network of lakes and canals as so many have since 1876. The St. Louis World's Fair was located at this park setting, and the waterways were a major focus of the Fair's landscape.

This popular lunch spot features a Salmon BLT Sandwich served on sourdough bread and then lathered with basil mayonnaise. The famous Boathouse Blue Cheese Slaw accompanies the sandwich. Chef Gregory Becker says it's a real favorite.

The Boathouse recently received a makeover inspired by midwestern boathouse cottages of the early twentieth century.

WHAT ELSE IS ON THE MENU? Sunday Brunch features Flank Steak and Eggs Rarebit

WHAT'S NEARBY? The Muny Opera and Saint Louis Zoo

HOW DO I GET THERE? From I-40, Hampton Ave. exit, take Washington Ave. to Government Dr.

HOW TO CONTACT 314-961-7588 | www.boathouseforestpark.com

College Town's Baby Burgers

Big is not always better. BOOCHES BILLIARD HALL in Columbia touts "USA's top burger" in 2000. Then in 2005, Booches was named "the best home dining." The Booches Burgers are small but mighty. The cheeseburger favorite is covered with grilled onions. You'd better order three or four, though, because no French fries are served. You'll have to settle for chips. Oh, and did I mention the burgers are served on wax paper instead of plates?

Another attraction and memory-maker is its Old World Billiard Hall that has entertained many a student and local as they chowed down on burgers and swigged one of the many choices of beer.

When students come back to their college town, Booches is their first stop. Businessmen make this a regular visit. Until 1970, this fun eatery served only men!

WHAT ELSE IS ON THE MENU? Homemade Chili and Soup

WHAT'S NEARBY? Downtown Columbia with retail shopping

HOW DO I GET THERE? 110 S. 9th St.; 10 to Paris Road to N. College (763) to E. Broadway to 9th St.

HOW TO CONTACT 573-874-9519

Smell the Rolls

Cinnamon rolls at the ROLLING PIN BAKERY in Glasgow have an aroma guaranteed to whet your appetite, whether it's breakfast time or not.

Jeremy Saylor, Rolling Pin's baker and owner, starts the rolls the night before baking. He lets the dough refrigerate overnight then removes it from the fridge in the morning to allow it to rise. After they are popped out of the oven, they measure five inches wide and two inches high. The icing glaze is the final touch of perfection. Dozens and dozens are made daily, along with the bakery's many pies and cheesecakes.

One of the unique features of this historic bakery is the collection of rolling pins displayed in the windows. These pins have accumulated through the years from their many customers.

Whether you are there for breakfast or lunch, you have the option of eating on their outdoor patio overlooking a fountain.

WHAT ELSE IS ON THE MENU? Great Homemade Chicken Salad

WHAT'S NEARBY? The Riverport Market Gallery

HOW DO I GET THERE? 104 Market St.; I-70 to Exit 121 toward Fayetteville, then M-240, right to Market St.

HOW TO CONTACT 660-338-0800

German Prime Rib

DAS STEIN HAUS in Jefferson City offers a total German dining experience from the décor to the wait staff in lederhosen to the traditional German food. A favorite dish is Beef Rouladen, which will surely melt in your mouth. Their staple menu item has two generous slices of prime rib basted with *Duesseldorfer Loewensenf*, an imported mustard from the Rhineland. The beef is then stuffed with dill pickles and onions and baked until tender. A rich mushroom sauce is delicately poured on top.

To complete the ethnic theme, you must have the German potatoes, which are crispy and moist with tangy red cabbage. How about those Missouri Germans!

Traditional German music and dancing, plus an incredible beer and liquor selection and the 150 different wines displayed on the wall, will enhance your German accent! *Guten Appetit!*

WHAT ELSE IS ON THE MENU? Bavarian Ice Cream with Strawberry Liquor

WHAT'S NEARBY? Missouri's State Capitol

HOW DO I GET THERE? 1436 Southbridge; I-54 to Jefferson, right on Zumbehl, to Southbridge

HOW TO CONTACT 573-634-3869 | www.dassteinhaus.com

See You in the Funny Pages

Eating in a restaurant can be more fun than you think. Bud Casey in Moberly took a humorous idea in 2003 and brought the funny pages to life in his FUNNY PAGES CAFÉ. Familiar characters like Beetle Bailey and Blonde are painted on the building's interior and exterior. A cartoon train encircles the building.

Many terrific choices populate the menu for breakfast or lunch, but the serious "Junk Yard Dog" is a breakfast that is funny in name but built for a serious appetite! A single biscuit is covered with three scrambled eggs and a layer of hash browns before white pepper gravy covers your plate. Smoked cheddar is sprinkled on top, with two slices of crispy bacon on the side.

Want to hear a good joke to add to your fun? Funny Pages has a new one for you every time you visit.

WHAT ELSE IS ON THE MENU? Seasoned French Dip Sandwiches

WHAT'S NEARBY? Little Dixie Regional Library

HOW DO I GET THERE? 217 N. 4th St.; Hwy. 63 to Rt. EE west to 4th St.

HOW TO CONTACT 660-263-5233

Just Say Cheese!

SWEETIE PIES, with two locations in St. Louis, has earned a reputation for its amazing southern Mississippi–style soul food. The *St. Louis Post-Dispatch* declared it the best soul food in town! The Food Network also featured Sweetie Pies on its *Diners, Drive-ins and Dives* show.

What you might not expect to find there is outstanding Macaroni and Cheese. Individually baked servings of this rich, buttery noodle dish are yours if you just say "cheese." Linda Montgomery, sister of Sweetie Pies owner Robbie Montgomery, says it is a secret recipe created by their mother that contains four different cheeses. But don't ask about its ingredients! Large quantities of the macaroni and cheese are made daily at their two locations. No alcoholic drinks are served, but great lemonade is waiting for you.

While you are there, ask to meet Robbie, who was once a nationally known backup singer. Ten other family employees have helped put Sweetie Pies on the map!

WHAT ELSE IS ON THE MENU? Smothered Pork Steaks

WHAT'S NEARBY? Tower Grove Park is one mile from The Grove location

HOW DO I GET THERE? 9841 Manchester off Chambers Rd.; and 4270 Manchester, two blocks east of Kingshighway

HOW TO CONTACT 314-521-9915 Florissant | 314-371-0304 The Grove

Dining at the Duck

A lakefront dining experience at the Lake of the Ozarks is indeed a treat unto itself, but to dine at THE DUCK is extra special. Donna Ziegler and Mark Hooter go out of their way to provide an extensive menu and special events.

It is no surprise that you will find Duck a L'Orange as one of its popular entrées. The plump duck breast is pan seared and served with orange liqueur sauce and the chef's own demi-glace. The most popular sides are garlic mashed potatoes and carrots with sherry sauce.

Since the Duck has earned the Wine Spectator and Wine Enthusiast Award, you can count on its thorough selection of California wines.

If you choose to arrive by boat from the lake, a dock is provided for your convenience. Plan your visit Wednesday through Sunday only.

WHAT ELSE IS ON THE MENU? Rosemary Rack of Lamb

WHAT'S NEARBY? Lake of the Ozarks and Bagnell Dam

HOW DO I GET THERE? 67 Cherokee Ct.; Hwy. 54 to Bagnell Dam, Exit to HH, 4 miles to Cherokee

HOW TO CONTACT 573-365-9973 | www.theduckrestaurant.com

29

Wild Game Adventure

TONANZIO'S in New Bloomfield is a restaurant not to be missed if you want to explore new flavors and unusual fare like wild pheasant, braised elk, buffalo sirloin, oxtail soup, and exotic seafood.

A popular, unique item on the menu is the Alligator Tail, which is brought in from the wild from the state of Louisiana. These alligators—which average eight and a half feet in length and two hundred pounds—offer tasty meat from the side of the jaws or from the tenderloins out of the tail.

Tonanzio's is located in Cedar Lake Lodge, where many of the rooms feature turn-of-the-century décor. For an out-of-the-ordinary dining experience, the Safari Room offers a jungle atmosphere.

Tom Dawson and his son Drake hunt and travel extensively to bring you the best game for their menu. At least three kinds of game are offered depending on their availability.

What a wild dining experience this can be!

WHAT ELSE IS ON THE MENU? Great Italian Pastas

WHAT'S NEARBY? Beautiful countryside and Cedar Lake

HOW DO I GET THERE? 8285 State Rd.; I-70 to Rt. J and go 17 miles

HOW TO CONTACT 573-491-3668; toll free 866-491-3668 | www.tonanzios.com

German Apple Butter and More

One of the more scenic and historic spots in our beautiful state is the small town of Frohna. The SAXON MEMORIAL, where German Lutherans arrived from Bremen and started the first Lutheran College, is tucked away in green rolling hills.

Every year a fall festival is held during the second week in October. The festival celebrates all the German food specialties that maintain the German culinary heritage.

Apple Butter is made outdoors alongside an oven that turns out fresh baked bread at a rapid pace. German coffee cake is served along with the butter and bread. You can buy the bread by the slice and choose apple butter, homemade molasses, or cooked cheese to spread on it. German cooked cheese is like no other you have tasted.

Buggy rides, a farmer's market, crafters, and a costume contest makes Frohna's festival tops in the state!

WHAT ELSE IS ON THE MENU? Fresh Grilled Pork Burgers

WHAT'S NEARBY? The Lutheran Heritage Museum in Altenburg

HOW DO I GET THERE? 296 Saxon Memorial Drive; Hwy. 61 to Rt. K

HOW TO CONTACT 573-824-5404 | www.saxonlutheranmemorial.com

Mexican Mansion

Missouri has 428 Mexican restaurants from which to choose, but you will never experience better food and ambience than the BARBOSA'S CASTILLO in St. Joseph.

It all started with Mama Barbosa making enchiladas for her friends. In 1960, the family began serving authentic Mexican dishes to the public. Now Barbosa's has two locations in St. Joseph.

Enchiladas are still a favorite, although the tacos are frequently mentioned because of their hand-made shells. The soft and hard shells are filled with your choice of ground beef or chicken, plus all the usual fixings. Every recipe originates from south of the border, with a touch of North America for the flavors. "Taco Tuesdays" are a bargain, so mark your calendar.

This castle towers above downtown St. Joseph and has a fantastic view of the city. For a romantic touch, ask to dine on the rooftop garden. *Muy Bueno!*

WHAT ELSE IS ON THE MENU? Margarita Mondays—Six Varieties to Choose From

WHAT'S NEARBY? Queen of Apostles Catholic Church

HOW DO I GET THERE? 906 Sylvanie St.; 229 to 9th to Sylvania St.

HOW TO CONTACT 816-233-4970 | www.barbosasrestaurant.com

How About a Pig Salad

CHUBBY'S BARBEQUE in Hayti has created a combination of its customers' favorite menu items, barbeque and salad. The famous Pig Salad is a thirty-two-ounce salad bowl filled with lettuce, red cabbage, tomatoes, and carrots. The salad is then topped with delicious hickory-smoked barbeque. Their fresh barbeque is made in a pit each and every day.

Sheila Greenwell, the restaurant's owner of eighteen years, says the salad is more than one person can eat, so it is a meal in itself, and then some!

The love for pigs permeates the restaurant. Nearby farmers and customers generously share their pig memorabilia for Greenwell's décor. Sheila has even designed Chubby's Barbeque tee shirts that you can purchase as a souvenir. Sounds like "Pig Heaven" to me!

WHAT ELSE IS ON THE MENU? Chopped Pork Sandwiches

WHAT'S NEARBY? Pemis Scott Memorial Hospital

HOW DO I GET THERE? 935 E. Washington St. I-55, to Hwy. 84, to E. Washington

HOW TO CONTACT 573-359-1450

3 Brothers of Labadie

The small community of Labadie does not appear on most maps, but many locals and tourists know about its 3 BROTHERS RESTAURANT AND BAR. John, Joe, and Tom Yarbrough opened this unique restaurant, with each brother adding his own expertise. They even convinced their parents to move to Labadie to enjoy their efforts and to lend a hand.

The owners have fresh seafood flown in on Fridays for a weekly fish fry. The restaurant also is popular for flexing its mussels, which arrive fresh from Penco, Alaska, and Nova Scotia. The savory appetizer is listed on their menu as Penco Mussels. Fifteen to twenty husked and cleaned mussels are hand picked and prepared in a hot skillet and cooked to order. A roasted tomato sauce is combined with wine and garlic broth to provide the unique flavor. A grilled sliced baguette accompanies this treat, ready for dipping.

The atmosphere is contemporary for this historic structure, a one-time post office that should generate plenty of conversation.

<u>WHAT ELSE IS ON THE MENU?</u> Fresh Grilled Vegetable Risotto

<u>WHAT'S NEARBY?</u> The Hawthorne Inn

<u>HOW DO I GET THERE?</u> 117 Front St.; I-44 to Gray Summit to Hwy. 100 to Rt. MM to Hwy. T then left to Front St.

<u>HOW TO CONTACT</u> 866-577-3468

From Italy to Greenwood

In 1902, the Perazelli family arrived in America. Generations later, the family continues its tradition of Italian recipes in PERAZELLI'S Restaurant, located in the bedroom community of Greenwood. The restaurant is now situated in what was formerly a church, complete with customer seating in the choir loft.

Chicken Spiedini is one of the highlights of their extensive dinner menu. Marinated chunks of chicken are grilled and tipped with lemon butter sauce and a hint of red pepper.

Perazelli's also is known for its Italian bakery located on the lower level. The bakery also produces goodies for Perazelli's sister restaurant, Ciao! Bella, in Lee Summit. The carrot cake has been called the best in the state. This too is an old recipe made with heavy spices.

This family tradition of authentic Italian food is what you can expect and grow to love at Perazelli's.

WHAT ELSE IS ON THE MENU? Tiramisu

WHAT'S NEARBY? Antique shopping

HOW DO I GET THERE? 509 West Main St.; Hwys. 50, 291, 150 to Main St.

HOW TO CONTACT 816-537-9997 | www.perazellis.com

Brunch on the Bluffs

LES BOURGEOIS VINEYARD AND RESTAURANT sits high on the bluffs of the Missouri River in Rocheport. The winery is located in an A-frame building with seating available on a multi-tiered patio and landscaped garden overlooking the river and the Katy Trail. The restaurant is a short walk from the winery and offers expansive and breathtaking views from its generous windows.

Sunday brunch is a great dining choice, along with the award-winning wine. The breakfast items—such as the four-ounce tenderloin with eggs—are carefully chosen by the chef. Unusual sandwiches such as the grilled mahi mahi are on the brunch menu because they can easily be included in a picnic lunch—a romantic idea to be sure!

Save room for a dessert to die for! Vanilla sponge cake with orange honey mousse and ice cream topped with chocolate sauce will create a lasting memory of Les Bourgeois.

WHAT ELSE IS ON THE MENU? Beef Tenderloin (Dinner Menu)

WHAT'S NEARBY? The Katy Trail at the base of the bluff

HOW DO I GET THERE? 12847 West Hwy. BB; I-70 to BB

HOW TO CONTACT 573-698-2300 | www.missouriwine.com

A Businessman's Lunch

If you want to share a good lunch with the locals in a historic atmosphere, stop by the PEARL STREET GRILL in Harrisonville.

The businessman's favorite is the Pork Tenderloin Sandwich. The Rueben Sandwich rates a close second. The tenderloin is pounded for tenderness, lightly breaded, and then deep-fried. A touch of hearty horseradish, lettuce, tomato, and onion top this generous combination fit for any appetite.

Pearl Street Grill occupies a historic building in a historic area. Unique antique toys decorate the natural brick walls. A gyrocopter hangs from the ceiling, certain to catch your eye while eating lunch.

Manager Brian Bardo says the restaurant, which opened in 1979, is a place where everyone will want to meet and eat, whether it's the businessman's lunch or not!

WHAT ELSE IS ON THE MENU? A Hearty Breakfast Menu

WHAT'S NEARBY? The courthouse and local businesses

HOW DO I GET THERE? 207 E. Pearl St.; Hwy. 71 to Wall St. exit, go east 7 blocks to downtown

HOW TO CONTACT 816-380-1122

If It's Chicken, It's Galvin's

Since 1940, GALVIN'S DINNERHOUSE has been best known for its secret fried chicken recipe. Since owners Bill and Toni Grace took over, the chicken is now served family style, so you can eat your heart out! Bowls of mashed potatoes, gravy, corn, and green beans accompany each meal. Add a bowl of homemade soup, plus salad and hot rolls, and it feels just like Sunday dinner at Grandma's house.

A lovely atmosphere of white tablecloths, antiques, and festive lighting belie the building's former occupant—a Phillips Service Station.

It only gets better at Galvin's with *complimentary* desserts to all adult customers and *free* ice cream to children.

What could make a better dining experience for the whole family?

WHAT ELSE IS ON THE MENU? Braised Pork Chops (if you call ahead)

WHAT'S NEARBY? Half mile from Spring Garden Middle School

HOW DO I GET THERE? 6802 S. 22nd St.; half mile south of Hwy. 229 overpass

HOW TO CONTACT 816-238-0463 | www.galvinsstjoe.com

Hot Dog!

Hot dogs are a staple of every child's diet. We've all eaten and enjoyed them. If you are looking for the best hot dog in Missouri, head to Joplin, a town best known for its mysterious "spook lights," a centuries-old unexplained paranormal light.

Ten miles from these lights, DECKER'S BAR AND GRILL offers a dose of reality with ten different hot dog varieties to choose from. The Junk Yard Dog captures the most attention, consisting of polish sausage on a brat bun dressed with mustard, cheese sauce, chili, chopped lettuce, and onions, followed by a good dose of sauerkraut.

This cozy "dog house" seats only thirty people, but outdoor seating is also available right next to Shoal Creek. Owner Pam Beaver moved to Joplin from Florida, and the eatery reflects that fishing and tropical décor of her former home.

WHAT ELSE IS ON THE MENU? Onion Fried Petals with Dipping Sauce

WHAT'S NEARBY? Zane's Campground and Shoal Creek

HOW DO I GET THERE? 2487 Coyote Dr. between McClelland Park and Apricot St.; located on the corner of Apricot and Coyote

HOW TO CONTACT 417-623-8733

Out-of-the-Norm Dining

Who would expect to dine on Italian fare in a 1960s split-level located along the highway in Lebanon, Missouri? Gary Dyer, owner of GARY'S PLACE, bucks the norm with his popular sense of humor.

Influenced by the cooking of his Grandmother Bellini, once a famous chef in Italy, Gary names his menu items after her. The top seller is Grandma Bellini's Oven Roasted Lasagna. Why so great? Eleven layers of tasty sauces, pastas, sausage, and ground beef are meshed with four different cheeses: romano, parmesan, mozzarella, and ricotta. At least two hundred portions are served each week.

Three dining rooms and outside seating are located on the lower level, while a bed and breakfast occupies the second floor. Gary's Place also hosts a Murder Mystery several times a month. Check the website for additional information, including a wonderful photo of Gary's grandmother.

WHAT ELSE IS ON THE MENU? Gary's Chocolate Pies with Walnuts or Cashews

WHAT'S NEARBY? Atchley Park is 3 miles away, 2 miles north of city limits

HOW DO I GET THERE? 27819 Hwy. 5; I-44 to Exit 129 (Jefferson St.) to Hwy. 5

HOW TO CONTACT 417-532-0340 | www.garysitalianplace.com

Catfish Family Style

Catfish is a Missouri tradition and treat. A visit to DADDY JIM'S in Neosho provides a down-home, family style catfish meal at its best. The restaurant is named after owner Chuck Craig's father.

Chuck's secret to a "non-fishy"–tasting fish is to bread it in fine Shawnee white corn meal, then deep fry it in pure peanut oil. With sixteen sides available, it's hard to choose, but Chuck said hush puppies, mashed potatoes, and applesauce are the favorites.

The walls of Daddy Jim's are filled with memorabilia, including military and family photos, flags, souvenirs, and anything else you would like Chuck to display.

There is a lot of cooking going on when you feed twelve hundred customers a week. Their customers go back five generations, so the menu reflects many choices. The place is friendly, fun, and very fishy!

WHAT ELSE IS ON THE MENU? Steaks that Melt in Your Mouth!

WHAT'S NEARBY? Crowder College 1 mile away

HOW DO I GET THERE? 16202 Hwy. 59; I-44 to Hwy. 71 to Neosho/ Seneca Exit to Hwy. 59

HOW TO CONTACT 417-455-0882

World's Fair Sundae

Nine years after the 1904 St. Louis World's Fair, the CROWN CANDY KITCHEN opened in St. Louis by Harry Karandzieff and his buddy Pete Jugaloff. They both had confectionary skills from Greece that helped create one of the most famous landmarks in Missouri. Crown Candy still is run by the Karandzieff brothers.

Fourteen or more sundae specials are listed on their sinfully delightful menu, including the French Sundae, the real enchilada of sundaes! It has three sauces, strawberry, pineapple, and marshmallow, ladled over two scoops of vanilla ice cream, surrounded by sliced bananas. The toppers are whipped cream, crushed cashews, chocolate sprinkles, and, of course, a cherry!

This cozy, historic structure still features the store's original wooden booths, checkerboard floor, and display counters. Also be sure to check out all the thirty-one varieties of homemade candy.

WHAT ELSE IS ON THE MENU? Homemade Egg Salad Sandwiches

WHAT'S NEARBY? 1½ miles from the Gateway Arch

HOW DO I GET THERE? 1401 St. Louis Ave.; I-70 to
Florissant Rd. to St. Louis Ave.

HOW TO CONTACT 314-621-9650 | www.crowncandykitchen.net

42

A Meal
All in One

There is nothing yummier among comfort foods than a good baked potato that is fresh, hot, steamy, and loaded! The Ory Spud is one popular entrée aside from barbeque that is being served at the MISSOURI HICKS BARBEQUE in Cuba, Missouri. This whopping potato is split and popped open for barbeque baked beans, pulled pork, Monterey Jack cheese, bacon bits, collards, Montreal seasoning, and a topping of sour cream. This is truly a meal in itself!

When you walk into this primitive Western-style building, you will see homemade cedar tables and chairs, as well as restrooms that look like authentic "out houses." Old implements and rustic paraphernalia will take you back in time. Active railroad tracks across the street only enhance the feeling of being in the Old West. Many know this stretch of road as part of the old Route 66.

WHAT ELSE IS ON THE MENU? Barbeque Brisket with
Ozark Salad

WHAT'S NEARBY? The Old Sisco Train Station

HOW DO I GET THERE? 913 E. Washington; Right off Hwy. 19
and I-44

HOW TO CONTACT 573-885-6791

A Gathering for Filets

MCGURK'S PUBLIC HOUSE in O'Fallon is a regular gathering place where you can feast your eyes on historic woodwork or a beautiful garden patio.

The locals will tell you that McGurk's does many things well, but perhaps nothing is better than its thick, tender, and mouth watering grilled Black Angus Filet Mignon. The menu suggests sides of Yukon Gold mashed potatoes, green beans, and carrots with a Madeira glaze. No matter how rare or well done, the filet represents the best of McGurks!

This stately building was built in 1862, when Frederick Westhoff founded the Westhoff Mercantile. After various uses, including the place where O'Fallon's first newspaper debuted, it found its pulse in the community as a public eatery.

A hand-carved wooden bar greets you as you enter. The stained glass throughout the restaurant is from an abandoned church. Local elected officials frequent McGurk's after council meetings that take place across the street.

WHAT ELSE IS ON THE MENU? Flourless Chocolate Cake with Tahitian Ice Cream and Raspberry Caulis

WHAT'S NEARBY? O'Fallon's Police Station and City Hall

HOW DO I GET THERE? 108 S. Main St.; I-70 to Exit 217 to Main St.

HOW TO CONTACT 636-978-9640

Shake It Up at the 4th Street Fountain

Elsberry is home to only some two thousand people, but generations have grown up having an Ice Cream Shake at the 4th STREET FOUNTAIN, established in the 1940s. This historic charmer has hosted many businesses prior to Wes and Marcia Fakes purchasing the building and restoring its unique features, including counters, stools, floors, and ceiling fans.

The soda jerks will tell you about the many delicacies, but the shakes sell more steadily than anything else. They credit the rich and creamy Serendipity Ice Cream. There are twelve kinds of shakes to choose from, and they come in three sizes. Chocolate, of course, remains the top seller. Everything gets topped with whipped cream—thank you, thank you.

Not to worry if you are dieting, however, because the thin mint shakes are made with fat-free and sugar-free ice cream, with a touch of mint abstract, topped off with a thin mint cookie. This healthy treat could fool anyone. All of the containers and décor are reminiscent of the 1950s, when this whole experience was indeed a treat. "Shake it up baby," as Elvis would say!

WHAT ELSE IS ON THE MENU? Cherry Cokes and Smoothies

WHAT'S NEARBY? Elsberry Park across the street

HOW DO I GET THERE? 401 Broadway; Hwy. 79 to the stop sign at Broadway and 4th St.

HOW TO CONTACT 573-898-9793 | www.4thstreetfountain.com

Crab Cakes in the Eagle's Nest

The little riverside town of Louisiana, Missouri, has much to offer besides being known as "bald eagle country." The EAGLE'S NEST is one place you will not want to miss when it comes to food, featuring a menu abundant with seafood.

The Louisiana Crab Cakes get great reviews both as an appetizer and as a main entrée. They are generous in stature and are served on an attractive lettuce plate with two dishes of smoked tomato sauce. Orange honey-glazed salmon or breaded catfish also are great entrées you may want to sample.

This eagle's nest also houses a bakery, winery, conference center, and overnight inn. How about a little education thrown into your visit? The Eagle's Nest's creative and knowledgeable owner, Karen Stuckley, hosts a culinary class called Provence Culinary Experience. She was once the food editor for *Missouri Life Magazine*. I would say we could all nest here for some time!

WHAT ELSE IS ON THE MENU? A Great Rack of Lamb

WHAT'S NEARBY? 3 blocks from Karen's husband's place, John Stuckley's Studio, famous for his sketches of Missouri.

HOW DO I GET THERE? 221 Georgia St.; I-70, Hwy. 79, to 3rd St. to Georgia St.

HOW TO CONTACT 573-754-9888 | www.theeaglesnest-louisiana.com

French Quarter, Missouri Style

Along the banks of the Mississippi River in the heart of Cape Girardeau is a romantic restaurant that takes you back to Louisiana's famous French Quarter. The ROYAL N'ORLEANS RESTAURANT is located in a historic building that used to be the town's opera house. Restored in 1990 after a couple of fires, the restaurant now offers French cuisine and Cajun dishes.

Be sure to check out the Chateaubriand, a prepared tenderloin beef cut placed on a silver platter with a medley of vegetables. Before serving, the combination is set aflame and carried to your table where hot garlic whipped potatoes are waiting. The waiter serves mouth-watering portions directly from the platter.

Derek Miller, the proprietor, goes out of his way to create the festive New Orleans décor. Outdoor lampposts, fencing around the balcony level, plus formal white tablecloths create an elegant, Southern dining experience. Piano music from the bistro/bar entertains diners on Friday and Saturday nights. All this without leaving the state of Missouri!

WHAT ELSE IS ON THE MENU? Crème Brûlée

WHAT'S NEARBY? Across the street from the *Southeast Missourian Newspaper*

HOW DO I GET THERE? 300 Broadway St.; I-55 to Exit 99 East, take Hwy. 34, left to Broadway

HOW TO CONTACT 573-335-8191 | www.royalnorleans.com

The Best for Last in Fine Dining

I say we start with dessert at CLARY'S RESTAURANT in Springfield, Missouri. Dessert is a must for every Clary's customer because of its well-earned reputation for homemade soufflés. Every-day fresh custard is made into a pastry cream by adding meringue, followed by the chosen flavor of the day. Chocolate is always on the menu, but popular favorites like amaretto, apricot, blueberry, and white chocolate espresso can be there waiting for you if you call ahead. There is no sense in trying this in your own home!

However, please don't ignore the extensive menu, which is largely influenced by freshly grown produce. You will even find fresh herbs in their backyard. James Clary knows local farmers, fishermen, and poultry owners who add to Clary's good food.

After that fantastic dessert, stop at their "waterfall bar" for an after-dinner drink. Fine dining in this college town is no doubt Clary's Restaurant.

WHAT ELSE IS ON THE MENU? 8-ounce Filet with Red Onion Jam Sauce

WHAT'S NEARBY? In the center of the Battlefield Market Shopping Center

HOW DO I GET THERE? 900 E. Battlefield; from the Glenstone exit, off Hwy. 60, go westbound; between National and Campbell Sts.

HOW TO CONTACT 417-886-6200 | www.eatatclarys.com

A Celebrity Breakfast

Staying at a bed and breakfast is always a delight, but when your food is prepared by a "Dierbergs Celebrity Chef," you are sure to be pleased. Cathy, the chef, and her husband, Carl McGeorge, own the LOGANBERRY INN, where celebrities have slept and dined, including Margaret Thatcher, England's former prime minister. This wonderful inn is located in Fulton, Missouri, where Winston Churchill gave his famous speech.

All of the delicious breakfasts begin with maple baked apples or cinnamon pears. Choose from among ten coffees, seven types of tea, and several kinds of juice. Most guests love the Eggs Florentine, a light and airy spinach soufflé served with caramel pecan waffles. A variety of French toasts, crepes, and quiches are served on fine china, always with a custom touch from Cathy.

In the winter, relax by a crackling fire, or enjoy tennis nearby in the summer. You never know which celebrity you might meet next.

WHAT ELSE IS ON THE MENU? Cathy's Special Baked Cookies

WHAT'S NEARBY? The Winston Churchill Memorial and Museum

HOW DO I GET THERE? 310 West 7th St.; 5 minutes from I-70

HOW TO CONTACT 573-642-9229 | www.loganberryinn.com

A Taste of Glenn's

Visiting historic Boonville, Missouri, is indeed an experience in many ways. One of the keystones, Hotel Frederick, is right in the heart of town. It is a charming boutique hotel with a world-class restaurant called GLENN'S CAFÉ. This Romanesque Revival structure was built in 1905 by Charles A. Sombart, a local miller and banker. In 2004, a major renovation took place, and the Frederick was put on the map with its new bar, lobby, guestrooms, and most of all Glenn's Café.

If you should start in the bar, try the raw oysters. Take your drink on the deck and overlook the beautiful Missouri River. A "Taste of Glenn's" on the menu is a good way to experience all that the café has to offer. Start with a cup of seafood gumbo and crawfish-andouille cake, chicken tchoupitoulas, blackened redfish, bronzed pork chop, smoked brisket, shrimp Creole, red beans and rice, and spaghetti squash. Finish it all off with bread pudding and whiskey sauce. Expect the wait staff to ask about your favorite.

WHAT ELSE IS ON THE MENU? Family Style Breakfast and Dinner on Sundays

WHAT'S NEARBY? Historic Thespian Hall and Boonville's business district

HOW DO I GET THERE? Main and High Sts.; Hwy. 40 to Main to High

HOW TO CONTACT 660-882-9191 | www.glennscafe.biz

The Biggest Pancake Ever

Branson entertains millions of visitors each year as one of Missouri's top tourist destinations. Many travelers know where you can get a great breakfast with pancakes the size of a hubcap. Yes, you read it correctly, a hubcap. Gail Blong, owner of BILLY GAIL'S CAFÉ, says the pancakes are so big, they hang over the side of the plate. Order more than one at a time at your own risk. These cakes are paper thin and are very popular with blueberries or pecans. Don't be in a hurry, though, because only three

PANCAKE PATTY

pancakes fit on the grill at one time. Meat sides are available if you think you have room.

Billy Gail's is in an Ozarks country setting in a 1960s log cabin. Its interior is charming with red and white checkered tablecloths and red geraniums. It only seats fifty-six people, so get there early to get your pancake order in.

<u>WHAT ELSE IS ON THE MENU?</u> Texas-Size French Toast

<u>WHAT'S NEARBY?</u> 1 mile from Silver Dollar City

<u>HOW DO I GET THERE?</u> 5291 State Hwy. 265; Hwy. 65 to 465,
76, make left to 265

<u>HOW TO CONTACT</u> 417-338-8883

Goody Goody for You!

Patrons have been dining at the GOODY GOODY DINER in St. Louis since 1948. The diner originated from a local root beer stand and grew into one of the more popular breakfast spots in Missouri.

Breakfast with a capitol B is served until two in the afternoon. Unusual combinations like the Waffle with Fried Chicken or the Catfish and Eggs are just some of the hot dishes popular among regulars. Hash browns prepared in special popcorn butter and seasoning and topped with cheese and bacon are likely to show up as part of your meal.

The 1950s style of enjoying your meal in a vintage booth, bar stool, or checkered tabletops is straight out of the movies. Celebrities and politicians like Al Gore and Cedric the Entertainer have had the pleasure of dining at this famous eatery. The photo mural of the diner's past is not to be missed and provides a glimpse into the heart and soul of its history. Owners Richard and Laura Connelly are as attentive to every detail on the menu as the nostalgic décor.

WHAT ELSE IS ON THE MENU? Frosty Cold Root Beer in a Mug

WHAT'S NEARBY? 3 miles from Forest Park

HOW DO I GET THERE? 5900 Natural Bridge; off I-70 and Goodfellow

HOW TO CONTACT 314-383-3333 | www.goodygoodydiner.com

Seafood Dining for St. James

St. James is known nationwide for its Amish Community and beautiful countryside, but the town's offerings don't end there. Tom and Janet Scheffer, along with their daughter and son-in-law, combined their past experiences in the gift and restaurant businesses to open SYBIL'S ST. JAMES.

From an addition to an old farmhouse completed in 2007, the Scheffers created an elegant atmosphere where you can enjoy some of their enticing seafood. The Cashew Crusted Mahi Mahi with chopped tomatoes and cucumber remoulade is outstanding! Basil Pesto Baked Sea Bass is another tempting choice. Can't decide? Enjoy the Surf n' Turf. Missouri wines are featured among the other choices.

While you enjoy your meal, take time to admire all the attractive antiques and gifts for sale and even use this opportunity to dine and shop. Sunday brunch is popular at Sybil's, so call early to make your reservation.

WHAT ELSE IS ON THE MENU? Bacon-Wrapped Maple Dijon Scallops

WHAT'S NEARBY? St. James Winery

HOW DO I GET THERE? 14502 Hwy. 68; 1-½ miles north of I-44

HOW TO CONTACT 573-265-4224

American as Apple Pie

Central to both the United States and the state of Missouri, you will encounter a truly American restaurant of some twenty years, owned by former school teachers Ron and Nicki Hopson. Plain and simple with no frills, SLICE OF PIE offers up good food at good prices in Rolla, Missouri.

There is no question what Slice of Pie is known for from across the state. Just name your favorite pie, because there are over thirty varieties to choose from. If you cannot decide, order a "sample pie," which gives you small slices of your favorites. It is probably no surprise that American Apple Pie is the best seller. The flaky crust holds eight cups of sliced apples in each pie, each weighing in at an impressive seven pounds. The top is coated with a special cinnamon frost generously drizzled over each piece. You may have to pass on that scoop of ice cream, because the slice alone is a challenge to eat.

In addition to the pies, Slice of Pie offers a lunch menu. The restaurant seats only twenty-five people, so takeout orders are popular in this college town!

WHAT ELSE IS ON THE MENU? Two Kinds of Chicken Salad

WHAT'S NEARBY? UMR, now S&T University

HOW DO I GET THERE? 601 Kingshighway; I-44 to Hwy. 63 to 6th St.; corner of 6th and Kingshighway

HOW TO CONTACT 573-364-6203

Missouri Goes Hawaiian

If you are looking for a Missouri nautical vacation along with the experience of tropical dining, visit the MARINA GROG AND GALLEY overlooking the water in Lake Lotawana. The backdrop is the largest private lake in the metropolitan Kansas City area. Restaurant owner Jack Schwindler enjoys the distinction of being the first baby born in this small town of eighteen hundred residents.

Hawaiian seafood has become a specialty according to Head Chef Amy Presson, who prepares Hawaiian Lobster served in a half roasted pineapple shell. The black Thai rice is the base for the sautéed lobster, scallops, and shrimp that are in the lobster cream sauce. Add fresh asparagus to round out a meal to remember. Each week the restaurant also features a special fish from Hawaii.

Unlike many lakefront restaurants, this galley is open year round seven days a week. Be sure to bring your camera for many photo opportunities, including Christmas, when every corner of the restaurant is covered in white lights!

WHAT ELSE IS ON THE MENU? Dry Aged Steaks

WHAT'S NEARBY? Lake Lotawana and Lake Jacomo

HOW DO I GET THERE? 1 Waters Edge; Hwy. 7 to Colbern Rd.
Gate 1 turn right

HOW TO CONTACT 816-578-5511 | www.marinagrogandgalley.com

Great Rolls If You Can Catch Them!

When you mention "unique eateries," everyone in Missouri wants to tell you about LAMBERT'S CAFE, home of the "throwed rolls." We don't necessarily want the rest of the United States to think we throw our food around, but in 1976, Lambert's developed a strange custom when Owner Norman Lambert walked around his restaurant serving hot rolls. When he could not serve them fast enough, his customers would yell out for him to just throw them the rolls, so he did! He continues to throw them today so customers won't be disappointed. This is entertainment you do not want to try in your own home!

The delicious five-inch round rolls are extra yummy with sorghum molasses. The oven turns out rolls continuously from 9:15 a.m. to 9:00 p.m. Lambert's serves about 520 dozen rolls per day for a total of over 2.2 million rolls per year.

Other good home cooking is offered in a large dining-room atmosphere, which easily accommodates large groups. There are three locations.

WHAT ELSE IS ON THE MENU? Cinnamon Rolls as big as hubcaps

WHAT'S NEARBY? Sikeston Outlet Mall

HOW DO I GET THERE? Sikeston: 2305 E. Malone St.; I-55, Hwy. 62 to Malone

HOW TO CONTACT 573-471-4261 | www.throwedrolls.com

Home Town Pizza

Generations have grown up in St. Charles enjoying the paper-thin crust pizza made at PIO'S ITALIAN RESTAURANT. Many traditional Italian dishes are popular at Pio's because of their Italian heritage, but most know that their signature item is pizza, and the third generation of the Dempsey family has been serving it in the community since 1955.

The word on the street, without disclosing too many secrets, is that their blend of many cheeses and cracker-thin crust are what make the pizza so unique. A variety of toppings are available, but pepperoni and onion and the special deluxe are the most frequent requests.

When Lindenwood College students leave or families move away and return to visit, Pio's has to be one their first stops. Many celebrations have been held at this vintage two-story corner restaurant, located on a hill overlooking the Missouri River and St. Charles historic area.

<u>WHAT ELSE IS ON THE MENU?</u> Homemade Soups and Crispy Fried Chicken

<u>WHAT'S NEARBY?</u> St. Joseph Medical Center/Hospital

<u>HOW DO I GET THERE?</u> 403 First Capitol Dr.; I-70 go north to First Capitol Dr.

<u>HOW TO CONTACT</u> 636-724-5919 | www.piosrestaurant.com

Miss Muffin's Brownies

You haven't tasted a brownie like the ones you can order at the LIL' MISS MUFFINS AND STUFF TEAROOM in Jackson, Missouri. Palmie Henry, the tearoom's owner, knows how popular the chocolate delicacy has become. The generous six-by-three-inch slice is loaded with chocolate chips and coated with chocolate gnash that begs to be accompanied by vanilla ice cream and served warm.

The tearoom is located in the Strickland Building in downtown Jackson. The owners conveniently live upstairs to dedicate themselves to the many hours of service and good product. The tearoom shares a hallway with the Cottage Quilt Shop of Jackson. Shoppers love buying their fabric and gifts and then treating themselves at the charming tearoom next door.

WHAT ELSE IS ON THE MENU? Teapot-Shaped Cakes

WHAT'S NEARBY? The Cape Girardeau County Court House

HOW DO I GET THERE? 113 West Main St.; I-55 to Kingshighway/ Jackson Blvd. to High St., then left on Main

HOW TO CONTACT 573-204-1933 | www.muffinandstuff.com

Meatloaf on Main Street

When you visit downtown Salem—which has much to offer including the Dent County Court House—good home cooking is waiting for you. Some may visit MAIN STREET CAFÉ on the center town square for their daily cup of coffee, but many flock to the restaurant to partake of America's favorite comfort food, meatloaf.

The generous two-by-four-inch serving, made from secret ingredients only known to longtime cook Barb Field, is covered in tomato sauce, served with gravy, and comes with a side of mashed potatoes. An unusual but favorite side is the pinto brown beans.

Owner Joyce Davis says her soups and chicken and dumplings are a town favorite. She keeps the country décor plain and simple because Main Street Cafe is all about the food!

WHAT ELSE IS ON THE MENU? Seven Different Homemade Pies

WHAT'S NEARBY? Seven blocks from Fiebleman's Antiques and Ozark Information Center

HOW DO I GET THERE? 509 N. Main St.; I-44 to Hwy. 19, which turns into Main St.

HOW TO CONTACT 573-729-5050

Baby Back Ribs in a Cave

We all enjoy a clever and unique atmosphere when we dine, but the food still has to be the main attraction. CAVEMAN BARBEQUE AND STEAK HOUSE in Richland accomplishes both, without disappointing.

David Hughes and his wife, Connie, decided almost fifteen years ago that a restaurant located fifty feet above the road at a former campground would be an attraction no one would want to miss. When you arrive at this location, you are shuttled to an elevator and transported to a cave in a bluff above the Gasconade River. Dehumidifiers are used to keep the air inside a comfortable 69 degrees.

The Hugheses put a lot of effort in preparing their Baby Back Ribs, made with secret ingredients that keep customers coming back. If the whole or half slabs are not a meal unto themselves, pair them with a salad and baked potato side.

WHAT ELSE IS ON THE MENU? Many Cuts of Steak

WHAT'S NEARBY? The countryside and Gasconade River

HOW DO I GET THERE? 26880 Rochester Rd.; I-44 to Hwy. 7 north, then right on Rochester Rd.

HOW TO CONTACT 573-765-4554 | Closed Monday–Wednesday

Wabash Railroad Barbeque

Chillicothe is known as the "home of sliced bread," because the first bread slicer was invented here. WABASH BARBEQUE offers plenty to place on that sliced bread. The Chillocothe location is the second of two Wabash Barbeques. The "mother store" is located in Excelsior Springs, where Jim and Cheri McCullough purchased the Wabash Railroad Depot in 1997, restored it, and created the eatery of conversation.

Their smoked choices of turkey, ham, pulled pork, brisket, sliced pork, baby ribs, and spare ribs all are served with their secret-recipe Wabash Sauce. The hickory flavor is offered in regular or hot. The barbeque is served with sides called "switches or signals."

The depot has railroad memorabilia and original photos throughout the restaurant, and the outdoor Blues Garden is great on Saturday nights, when you are likely to hear music along with your cold beer and barbeque.

WHAT ELSE IS ON THE MENU? Hickory Smoked Chicken With Fries

WHAT'S NEARBY? Downtown Chillicothe

HOW DO I GET THERE? Chillicothe: 1 Elm St.; Hwy. 65 to Elm St.

HOW TO CONTACT 660-646-6777 for Chillicothe Depot | 816-630-7700 for Excelsior Springs Depot | www.wabashbbq.com

Thai Food on the River

COOPER'S LANDING is an all-inclusive experience on the Missouri River's edge. You can pull up in your boat or car to this eatery that offers the best in Thai food or tasty barbeque. Most of the Thai food is cooked in a trailer, called Chum's Thai Kitchen, parked next to the landing's gathering room. Service to the landing is provided from March through October. Pad Thai in peanut sauce and the Pad Pak Ruam Mitre, which is stir-fried mixed vegetables with your choice of meat, are the most popular dishes offered. Lewis and Clark, who also walked along this trail, would have welcomed something to eat besides the food nature had to offer.

Mike Cooper, the owner and creator of this multi-use recreational facility, wanted to offer Katy Trail riders and boaters unique food as well as outdoor musical entertainment. Once a bait and tackle shop more than twenty years ago, it is now a destination for many travelers. In the winter, Cooper's Landing is the place to go to watch bald eagles and witness sea gulls catching fish in the river.

WHAT ELSE IS ON THE MENU? A Hot Breakfast Menu

WHAT'S NEARBY? Missouri River and boat marina on the premises

HOW DO I GET THERE? 11505 Smith Hatchery Rd.; I-70 to 63 to 163 to S. Easley

HOW TO CONTACT 573-657-2544 | www.cooperslanding.net

Custom-Made Wine Cream

WINE COUNTRY GARDEN AND NURSERY in Defiance has been widely known for its extensive nursery in a park-like setting. Five acres of daylilies will amaze you, and a darling garden gift shop is sure to tempt you as well.

Good food and wine has recently been the garden's feature, as many enjoy dining around the lake or on porches and patios. Themed dinners, Friday night barbeques, and even picnic basket lunches are popular options among patrons.

Wine tastings include an extensive wine list and a delightful dessert that combines ice cream and wine. It is a marriage that blends the tastes of real 14 percent butterfat ice cream from Serendipity Ice Cream Shop and your favorite wine selection. Each ice cream flavor contains up to 5 percent alcohol, so you must be twenty-one to enjoy it. Flavors like Pino Peach and Tawny Porto are elegantly served in trendy decorated wine glasses. Chris and Bill Shal, the garden's owners, live on the premises to make sure every detail in landscaping and dining is addressed to perfection.

WHAT ELSE IS ON THE MENU? Wonderful Chicken Salad Sandwiches

WHAT'S NEARBY? Charming small towns in the hills of wine country

HOW DO I GET THERE? 2711 S. Hwy. 94; west on Hwy. 94 east of Defiance, on top of the hill

HOW TO CONTACT 636-798-2288 | www.winecountrygardens.net

Liver Reigns Here!

The historic HOTEL STE. GENEVIEVE AND RESTAURANT is a monument in Ste. Genevieve, the oldest city in Missouri. The fourteen-room hotel and restaurant was built around 1900, and food and lodging have been the focus since its origin.

Many locals appreciate the Sunday family style dinners, which feature amazing and hard to find Liver Dumplings. The beef liver is mixed with ten ingredients to create the pencil-thin dumplings that are served with rich brown gravy. Sides of green beans and German sauerkraut complement their texture. Customers who typically don't like liver have been known to try these unique dumplings and have been surprised by their delicious flavor.

Jami Inman, owner for the past eleven years, also mentioned that one of the hotel's previous owners, the late Larry the spirit, is still around and helps out on occasion. He has been seen changing light bulbs and playing pranks on staff that casually accepts his presence. Room 14 is reserved for Larry, so beware!

WHAT ELSE IS ON THE MENU? Chicken Livers and Onions

WHAT'S NEARBY? Downtown businesses, including Sarah's Ice Cream Shop

HOW DO I GET THERE? Main and Merchant Sts.; Hwy. 61 to Market St., left on Main St.

HOW TO CONTACT 573-883-3562

The Challenge in Ethel, Missouri

Ethel has one hundred residents, a fire station, police station, post office, and the SANTA FE RESTAURANT. Ed Hutchinson bought the old Bank of Ethel building and converted it to a restaurant where people share tables and order from the wall-hung menu board.

The Challenge at the Santa Fe is a giant plate-size hamburger, complete with bun and your choice of condiments. It weighs in between twenty-two and twenty-four pounds. A salad and two pounds of fries come with this gigantic hamburger. Your dinner is *free* if you can eat it all! He offers this challenge annually, so be on the lookout for this fulfilling opportunity.

If you want to match the Challenge with a root beer float, then order the Moucho Grande, featuring two kinds of root beer and seven scoops of ice cream served in a large fish bowl.

Not to worry, average-size hamburgers and floats also are available. Keep in mind that the Santa Fe is open only Friday, Saturday, and Sunday, and closed in January and August (too hot and too cold). Are you up to the Challenge?

WHAT ELSE IS ON THE MENU? Pies and Banana Splits

WHAT'S NEARBY? Post Office and Public Services of Ethel

HOW DO I GET THERE? 101 N. Main St.; off Hwy. 149

HOW TO CONTACT 660-486-3334

65

Fried Bread

Teresa Leimkuehler of Morrison, Missouri, is from a family of twelve, so she grew up baking bread. Now, she and her husband make fried bread for their customers at their bar restaurant called HOP'S HIDEAWAY. They mix the dough, let it rise, roll it flat, then drop it in a deep fryer until golden brown. Each piece ends up being a different size and is complemented with homemade honey butter, making it a meal by itself!

The Leimkuehlers transformed a John Deere Tractor Store into a warm meeting place, featuring a beautiful 1900s cherry bar, carved by a blind, local craftsman. Conversation pieces abound throughout the Hideaway, including ten different mounted deer heads. Even though this hideaway is located in a remote area, everyone knows about it, and the bar/restaurant has become a destination unto itself.

WHAT ELSE IS ON THE MENU? Jumbo Fried Frog Legs

WHAT'S NEARBY? Farmland, no other businesses for six miles

HOW DO I GET THERE? 1106 Pershing Rd.; Hwy. 100 to Rts. N, J, OO to Pershing Rd.

HOW TO CONTACT 573-294-7126

1906 Centennial Pot Roast

The Keeter Center at the College of the Ozarks is a unique eating experience, because you are served by a staff of students at the DOBYNS DINING ROOM on the college campus. The students also contribute and market many of the creative menu items.

Food Manager Trent Starks boasts about the most popular menu item with students and guests alike: the 1906 Centennial Pot Roast, named to celebrate the college's first one hundred years. The choice beef is seared and braised for twelve hours before serving. Red skinned mashed potatoes and seasoned vegetables are perfect complements to this "taste of home, away from home." You are encouraged to finish off the meal with some of the students' home-baked desserts or real homemade ice cream.

You may want to visit the Keeter Center on Thursday or Saturday evenings, when the students provide entertainment with a variety of music. Special lodging and banquet accommodations also are available.

WHAT ELSE IS ON THE MENU? The Students' Pear Honey Salad Dressing, also available for sale

WHAT'S NEARBY? The Ralph Foster Museum

HOW DO I GET THERE? 1 Opportunity Ave.; Hwy. 65 S. through Branson to Hollister Interchange to Opportunity Ave.

HOW TO CONTACT 417-239-1900 | www.keetercenter.edu

Wine Cake When You Shop

Wine can make anything taste better, and at MAGGIE MAE'S TEA ROOM in Miller, Missouri, the Blackberry Wine Cake creates a tasty memory you will never forget. The red, dark texture is like no other flavored cake and is one of many unique desserts that complement the soups, quiches, and salads.

Maggie Mae's has seven dining room areas with themed décor, so eating and shopping are simultaneously competing for your attention. Choose from the Garden Room, Victorian Room, Terrace Room, Banquet Room, Library Room, Coke Room, and the newly decorated Tuscany Room.

Jack and Marsha Hill named their restaurant after a sign they saw near Kansas City, and the clever name combined their love of food and décor. Marsha says decorating is her love, but cooking is her work.

The town of Miller is only seven hundred people, but Maggie Mae's brings visitors from far and wide.

WHAT ELSE IS ON THE MENU? Seven-Layer Quiche

WHAT'S NEARBY? Half mile from town's activity

HOW DO I GET THERE? 206 E. 4th St.; I-44 to Hwy. 39 to 4th St.

HOW TO CONTACT 417-452-3299

Cajun Missouri Style

The RIVER'S EDGE RESTAURANT in Fredericksburg Village is housed in a former grist mill that the owner's ancestors built in the mid-1800s. Before turning into a full-fledged restaurant, during Prohibition the building reportedly ran a bootleg operation.

Today, a Cajun and Creole experience awaits those who order the Cajun Crab Boil for Two, an entrée that includes crab legs, crawfish, shrimp, and seafood gumbo. The gumbo—owner Linda Simon's personal recipe—is spicy, so you will be pleased to have the Flower Pot Baked Bread to calm the flames. If you are coming from Hermann, a five-minute ferry will float you across the Gasconade River to the River's Edge.

This restaurant could hold its own in the Big Easy, and food critics from *St. Louis Home and Garden* call the River's Edge one of Missouri's greatest dining treasures.

In Hermann, you will also want to try Simon's Restaurant, also located on the riverfront.

WHAT ELSE IS ON THE MENU? Charbroiled Showboat Shrimp

WHAT'S NEARBY? Gasconade River

HOW DO I GET THERE? 1720 Old Ferry Rd.; 9 miles from the mouth of the river

HOW TO CONTACT 573-294-7207 | www.simonswaterfrontrestaurants.com

Squeeze Inn for Tacos

After losing their restaurant in the town square of Stockton during a tornado in 2003, Ken and Ruth Noblett reopened THE SQUEEZE INN. Their reputation for great food comes from unique methods of preparation.

The Nobletts brought an original menu item back from a restaurant they once owned in California: grilled tacos. The whole corn tacos are grilled with meat and cheese and then opened up to add diced tomatoes, onions, and zesty salsa. Final touches include shredded cheese, sour cream, and a whopping order of fresh-cut French fries.

Squeezeburgers, BLTs, and Octopus Hotdogs are among the other popular favorites to try. You might ask Ken to serve up a cheese skirt grilled sandwich, which is crunchy around the edges.

Ken is sure to entertain you with his outrageous costumes and hats. His sense of humor and interesting décor throughout the inn is what keeps locals and new visitors alike coming back.

WHAT ELSE IS ON THE MENU? Ken's Caramel Apple Pecan Pie

WHAT'S NEARBY? half mile from Stockton Lake

HOW DO I GET THERE? 404 RB Rd.; Hwy. 13 to 32

HOW TO CONTACT 417-276-6302

Chili Parlor Extraordinaire

Did you know CASPER'S CHILI PARLOR is the oldest restaurant in Springfield, Missouri? It was originally located in a Quonset hut near downtown, and it still closes from Memorial Day to Labor Day.

Owner Belinda Harriman loves to boast about the chili recipe, which dates back to 1909. It is unique in that it does not contain tomatoes or onions, and the consistency is thicker than the average chili.

Casper Lederer opened the restaurant and passed it on to his son Charles, who died in 1985. Charles was quite the artist, and he painted the parlor in wild and crazy colors that continue to entertain people today. Unique collections of art and a wall menu will keep your eyes dancing, and exotic salt dough ornaments made through the years by Charlie are still displayed during Christmas.

Casper's Chili Parlor remains as popular today as it was when it opened one hundred years ago.

WHAT ELSE IS ON THE MENU? Hamburgers and Chili-Mac

WHAT'S NEARBY? Army Barracks

HOW DO I GET THERE? 601 West Walnut; I-44 to 13 to downtown

HOW TO CONTACT 417-866-9750

Chicken Bianco— A Must

Kirkwood is a lovely city of twenty-seven thousand people located in the suburbs of St. Louis, where Norman Rockwell would have felt right at home. MASSA'S Restaurant, situated in the heart of town, is one of the pulses of its business community.

Focusing on what menu selection would best represent the culinary experience at Massa's is challenging to say the least, until you hear about the Chicken Bianco—a chicken breast breaded just enough to have a slight crunch and topped with a wine and mushroom sauce. Massa's Italian Salad is a great introduction to the chicken, and the dressing is a secret combination of spices created by owner Jack Massa.

Jack and his co-owner brother Bill visit nightly and openly with customers. The Massas love to share stories about the building's history when it was the Vogt Funeral Home, and the staff can fill you in with many spiritual revelations! Massa's is decorated with a collage of color and flair. Two other locations are in Ellisville and Bridgeton.

WHAT ELSE IS ON THE MENU? Fried Artichoke Hearts

WHAT'S NEARBY? Kirkwood City Hall and Train Station

HOW DO I GET THERE? 131 W. Argonne off Kirkwood Rd./ Lindbergh Blvd.

HOW TO CONTACT 314-965-8050 | www.massasofcourse.com

The King of Ribs

Kansas City, Missouri, is known nationwide for its barbeque. The variety of barbeque is amazing, and the competition is strong. BRYANT'S BARBEQUE has earned its reputation over the years, and it has no equal when you are talking ribs!

The original restaurant was opened in the 1920s by Charlie Bryant, who worked with Henry Perry, the father of Kansas City barbeque. Bryant's brother Arthur took over when Charlie died. Arthur moved the restaurant four blocks away from Municipal Stadium, home to the Kansas City Chiefs. Three other locations soon followed.

The unique Arthur Bryant sauce has been enjoyed by celebrities and presidents, and the sauce recipes are closely guarded family secrets. The famous tender ribs are slowly smoked with a combination of oak and hickory, mellowed to the peak of flavor, and then basted with a rich and spicy sauce. If you love ribs, they are finger-licking good!

WHAT ELSE IS ON THE MENU? Tender Beef Brisket

WHAT'S NEARBY? East of the Jazz District in downtown K.C.

HOW DO I GET THERE? 1727 Brooklyn Ave.; I-70 to Hwy. 670, then 18th St. to Brooklyn

HOW TO CONTACT 816-231-1123 | www.arthurbryantsbbq.com

Ham It Up!

Missouri is fortunate to have a nationally known food producer located in California, Missouri. BURGERS' SMOKEHOUSE oversees production of two hundred thousand hams a year. They also produce bacon, sausage, and dozens of specialty meats. Steven Burger is the Smokehouse's fourth-generation owner.

Visitors who tour the smokehouse are greeted with a video of its history and other exhibits that explain the process of meat curing. The best part of the visit is actually sampling the many choices of meat sandwiches at their SMOKEHOUSE SANDWICH SHOP. After trying your favorite, chances are a cured ham or a pound or two of meat will find their way home with you.

On the third Saturday in September, you can feast and celebrate at the Ozark Ham and Turkey Festival, which supports the Cargill Turkey Plant and Burgers' Smokehouse, both located in California. This is a town with a lot of meat to it!

WHAT ELSE IS ON THE MENU? Summer Sausage and Smoked Turkey

WHAT'S NEARBY? The Moreau River

HOW DO I GET THERE? 32819 Hwy. 87; Hwy. 50 to 87, look for billboards

HOW TO CONTACT 800-345-5185 | www.smokehouse.com

A Scone to Remember

Tea rooms and bakeries across the country have scones on their shelves and menus, but the SHADY GABLES TEA ROOM in Versailles, Missouri, took scones to a new level when it created the Apricot, White Chocolate, and Black Missouri Walnut Scones. Each scone has a buttermilk base, making it light and airy, not dry and hard, as many others are. There are sixteen different flavors of scones to choose from in all.

This authentic English-style tea room offers etiquette classes for those unsure of how to behave in a formal eatery. Many awards and publications, including *Missouri Life Magazine,* have designated Shady Gables one of the top tea rooms in Missouri in 2006.

I am sure owner Reba Starling Silvey will be happy to arrange "scones to go" or a "scone tasting" if you ask. Leave it to the English!

<u>WHAT ELSE IS ON THE MENU?</u> Clotted Cream and Lemon Curd with Cream Tea

<u>WHAT'S NEARBY?</u> Doc's House specialty shops, across the street

<u>HOW DO I GET THERE?</u> 300 E. Newton St.; Hwy. 5, then 52 to Newton

<u>HOW TO CONTACT</u> 573-378-2740 | www.shadygables.com

Sausage Capital of Missouri

Hermann stakes claim to the title "Sausage Capital of Missouri." The city earned the title by celebrating WURSTFEST every fourth weekend in March. In 2009, they marked thirty years in the business of producing old-world delicacies.

THE STONE HILL WINERY PAVILION offers sausage-making demonstrations where you can sample Bratwurst, Liverwurst, and Summer Sausage. You can also purchase items from other sausage makers from all over Missouri.

HERMANOFF FESTIVAL HALL hosts professional and amateur sausage competitions. The five categories are Summer Sausage, Smoked Jerky, Smoke Stix, Exotic Fresh Sausage, and Exotic Sausage (cooked and smoked).

Musical entertainment and all the wineries Hermann has to offer make this a fun and tasty weekend.

WHAT ELSE IS ON THE MENU? A Variety of Wines and Cheeses

WHAT'S NEARBY? Antique shops in historic downtown Hermann

HOW DO I GET THERE? Junction 100 to 19

HOW TO CONTACT 800-932-8687 |
www.hermannmo.info:80/wurstfest/wurstfest.htm

A Honey of a Meal

If you are heading to the Lake of the Ozarks, you will want to schedule a stop in Greenville, where you will find TUPELO HONEY'S BAKERY AND CAFÉ, owned by Tiffanie and James Aitken.

Like most cafés, you will find a wide variety of sandwiches, but what is unique at Tupelo Honey's is their experimentation with food. An example is the Pot Pie, which comes in a casserole bowl with puff pastry topped with a scoop of mashed potatoes and gravy. Did you ever hear of a Catfish Poor Boy? What about a Puttanesca Omelet for breakfast? Tupelo Honey's specializes in both.

The sweet touch, however, comes from the fresh honey found at each table. The honey is shipped from the Apalachicola and Chipola river regions of northwest Florida. The Aitkenses, both professional chefs in their own right before opening Tupelo Honey's, like using honey whenever they can in their cooking and baking.

WHAT ELSE IS ON THE MENU? Chocolate Chip Peanut Butter Pie

WHAT'S NEARBY? Retail Shopping

HOW DO I GET THERE? 8779 N. State Hwy. 5; Hwy. 52 to Hwy. 5

HOW TO CONTACT 573-873-9955

Levi High Pie

I don't know if the BLUE OWL RESTAURANT in Kimmswick is in the Guiness Book of World Records, but it should be. Its pies are a sight to see and quite delicious, and the Carmel-Apple-Pecan Pie weighs eight pounds, is twelve inches high, and contains eighteen hand-sliced apples. Manager Kim Warner says the pie needs to be sliced cold to keep it from falling apart.

The Blue Owl has been featured twice on the Food Network, featuring many of its delicious delectables. A visit on Sunday means chicken and dumplings like grandma used to make. Roast beef and real mashed potatoes are another popular favorite.

In an atmosphere of blue and white décor, the Blue Owl carved out a spot on the map with its great pies and good home cooking, and owner Mary Hostetter should be very proud.

If you dare ask about the resident ghost, you'll have to ask the "pie makers" who work the night shift.

WHAT ELSE IS ON THE MENU? Pastry trays of twelve different desserts

WHAT'S NEARBY? Thirty specialty shops in a historic area

HOW DO I GET THERE? 2nd & Mill St.; I-55 to Exit 186 Main St. to town center

HOW TO CONTACT 636-464-3128 | www.theblueowl.com

Mardi Gras All Year Long

You don't have to go to New Orleans to experience authentic Cajun and Creole food. Tim Keller came to Dardenne Prairie after the flooding in New Orleans to open the LOUISIANA CAFÉ.

You must try the Crawfish Etouffee to get the "hurricane effect," which is quite spicy. Prepared crawfish are smothered in a roux-based gravy and vegetables that only Keller can create. This popular dish in New Orleans is dark in color and served over rice, but Keller says spicy does not mean "hot." Keller's expertise is received quite well in this small, booming community.

A Mardi Gras atmosphere dominates the restaurant, with an attractive New Orleans scene painted on one of the walls. Private parties are perfect in this café.

Tim claims his Louisiana Café is Cajun and Creole food from the soul.

WHAT ELSE IS ON THE MENU? Tim's Spicy Fried Chicken

WHAT'S NEARBY? Dardenne Town Square with theatre and shopping

HOW DO I GET THERE? 2698 Technology Dr.; off Hwy. 64/40

HOW TO CONTACT 636-561-8878 | www.louisiana-cafe.com

Fourth-Generation Coffee Cake

HOECKELE BAKERY AND DELI originated in 1937, but Paul and Joe Hoeckele of Perryville had no idea what a tradition they created. Now operating under fourth-generation ownership, the eatery's signature pastries are identified by the light and airy icing that only their staff has the privilege of knowing how to make. You will find this icing on their famous Peanut Butter Coffee Cake, a four-by-eight-by-one-inch cake with peanuts mixed into the icing. Because of the quantities sold, they are prepackaged and ready to go. Generations have grown up with this favorite, and many requests come from out of state to ship the cakes overnight.

After a long stint on Perryville's Court House Square, Hoeckele's moved to a brand new facility near the interstate, where it can now offer lunch and seating for customers.

The bakery has increased business on the thirteenth of every month, when visitors flock to a nearby Catholic seminary grotto and national shrine.

WHAT ELSE IS ON THE MENU? German Christmas Cookies

WHAT'S NEARBY? The National Shrine of Our Lady of the Miraculous Medal at St. Mary's of the Barrens Church

HOW DO I GET THERE? 1516 Edgemont Blvd.; a quarter mile from I-55, Exit 129

HOW TO CONTACT 573-547-4506

Old-Fashioned Soda Parlor

In Eminence, on your typical Main Street U.S.A., many old-fashioned tastes of food and fountain refreshments abound. Winnie Weber resurrected a historic building in 1999 to create the soda fountain/pharmacy she remembered as a child. WINFIELD'S will take you back in time when you see the ceiling fans, counters, stools, and turn-of-the-century soda and ice cream fountain.

You will find Winnie's favorites like pineapple Pepsi, cherry lemonade, fresh squeezed lemonade, and chocolate cake, which are now pleasing new generations.

The large building has living quarters for Winnie upstairs, along with other suites, and downstairs also accommodates an antique emporium with thirty dealers. The basement level houses the Rube's Roost, a charming old-time saloon.

If you are hungry, thirsty, or yearning to shop, Winfield's is the place to visit.

WHAT ELSE IS ON THE MENU? Open-Faced Sandwiches with Mashed Potatoes

WHAT'S NEARBY? Eminence Court House

HOW DO I GET THERE? 106 Main St.; take Hwy. 19 to Main St.

HOW TO CONTACT 573-226-3400 | www.winfields.com

Marvelous Mexican

Every community has its favorite local Mexican restaurant, and this is true of the happy patrons of EL JIMADOR Restaurant in Jefferson City. The Jefferson City location is the first of three, all of which are in the state capital.

Santa Fe Chicken is the number one choice on the menu, and this fairly spicy dish is grilled with bell peppers, onions, mushrooms, tomatoes, and topped with Jack cheese. A side of beans and rice accompanies it. The Santa Fe Chicken is served only on Thursdays and Mondays, so everyone can look forward to this special dish.

To make the meal complete, a Gold Margarita, made with special ingredients, has an extra shot of Grand Marnier. El Jimador is proud of its family friendly environment. Note this restaurant for your birthday, because you will be fitted with a sombrero while employees serenade you with their version of "Happy Birthday."

WHAT ELSE IS ON THE MENU? Fajitas Jimador with Sesame Seasoning

WHAT'S NEARBY? Jefferson Plaza Shopping Center

HOW DO I GET THERE? 1410 Missouri Blvd.; I-70 to Hwy. 54 to Missouri Blvd.

HOW TO CONTACT 573-761-1616

Enjoy Missouri's State Nut

The Eastern Black Walnut is Missouri's official state nut, and it grows best in the Missouri Ozark area. Expert nut tasters claim they are not too sweet and not too bitter.

HAMMONS BLACK WALNUT EMPORIUM in Stockton is home to the only black walnut processing plant in the United States. Packaged nuts, baked goods, and a variety of espresso and tea drinks mingled with clever gifts are great, but they are easily surpassed by the ice cream.

The three most popular black walnut ice cream flavors include caramelized black walnut, black walnut turtle, and basic black walnut ice cream. All three signature flavors are created for Hammons by Martin Dairy of Humansville, Missouri.

What better way to experience one of the "tastes of Missouri" than a scoop of black walnut ice cream on a cone? By the way, the ice cream cone is now officially one of the state's signature foods, since it was created at the St. Louis World's Fair in 1904. Tours are available, and the Black Walnut Festival is the third weekend in September.

<u>WHAT ELSE IS ON THE MENU?</u> Soups and Sandwiches

<u>WHAT'S NEARBY?</u> Businesses on the town square

<u>HOW DO I GET THERE?</u> 105 Hammons Dr.; I-44 to Hwy. 39, to to North St. to Hammons Dr.

<u>HOW TO CONTACT</u> 417-276-5800 | www.black-walnuts.com

Cobbler at Its Best

When we think of cobbler, we expect a great treat, and we may even think of the great cobbler favorite we grew up with. The Green Apple Cobbler, created by owner Brian Banhardt of Washington, Missouri, is made from scratch, and many wonder what the recipe might be. You will find this marvelous dessert at the AMERICAN BOUNTY RESTAURANT in a historic structure built in 1858 along the Missouri Riverfront, where the view is a major part of the dining experience.

The main course specialty at the Bounty is the hearty 9-Pasta dish, topped with pesto cream sauce, blackened chicken, black olives, scallions, and Roma tomatoes.

After dinner, visit the wine bar upstairs, or, weather permitting, the outdoor patio for a romantic finish to your evening. American Bounty also is known for fantastic catering.

WHAT ELSE IS ON THE MENU? Missouri and California Wines

WHAT'S NEARBY? Downtown Washington, along the Missouri River

HOW DO I GET THERE? 430 West Front St.; I-44 to Hwy. 100 to Hwy. 47 to river's edge

HOW TO CONTACT 636-390-2150

What's Hot in the Kitchen

Fayette is the proud home of EMMET'S KITCHEN AND TAP, where owner and chef Rob Schluckebier says Creole and Cajun food are about the celebration of food, drink, and music.

Shrimp Jambalaya is one of the best ways to celebrate at his restaurant, and the spicy flavor excites the tongue but does not numb it. Jambalaya is a versatile food using cooked rice with a variety of ingredients left to the chef's discretion. Adding shrimp and Rob's special seasonings make this is a pretty hot dish in more ways than one!

The jambalaya is served to perfection in a restored 1884 historic building, with décor that includes photography and art from local artist Ken Leigh.

Whether at Emmet's for events, private parties, or an evening out, you will be charmed by the restaurant and the community.

WHAT ELSE IS ON THE MENU? Big Easy Pasta Dish

WHAT'S NEARBY? Central Methodist University and antique shops

HOW DO I GET THERE? 111 N. Main St.; I-70 to Exit 40 to Hwy. 240 into Fayette

HOW TO CONTACT 660-248-3363 | www.emmetskitchen.com

Barbeque Since 1946

You just don't drive through Perryville without stopping at EWALD'S BARBEQUE, which opened as a car hop in 1946. Owned by Terry and Dottie Bucheit, Ewald's is the oldest restaurant in this friendly town.

Still only a "postage stamp"–sized restaurant in its original location, orders are taken at a counter just steps inside the door. There are only a few booths and a couple of tables, so many order their food to go. Larger quantities are available in pints, quarts, and even gallons, a popular practice among former Perryville residents wanting to take home some of their favorite memories of yesteryear.

The rave is all about Ewald's sliced hickory smoked barbeque pork, beef, and turkey, accompanied by a secret sauce with a hint of sweetness. Enjoy it on a traditional bun or toasted bread—the latter is most often preferred. Did I mention the sandwich sells for only $1.99?

WHAT ELSE IS ON THE MENU? Their Famous Malts, made the old-fashioned way

WHAT'S NEARBY? Two blocks from Perry County Court House Square

HOW DO I GET THERE? 18 E. North St.; I-55 to Hwy. 51 through Perryville to North St.

HOW TO CONTACT 573-547-8585

The Rueben Under the Cliff

THE UNDERCLIFF GRILL AND BAR features a unique eatery with eclectic décor unlike anything you have ever seen. Owners Melissa and Mike Winn created a restaurant built under one of Missouri's many cliffs, so relax and enjoy all the collected memorabilia displayed throughout the restaurant in its consistently cool interior. Originally a gas station and general store built in 1928, the site became a restaurant in 1961 but burned down. The Winns have brought it back to life with happy customers once again.

The Undercliff's popular Rueben Sandwich tops customer orders—a generous portion of corn beef stacked high, with grilled sauerkraut on top. Fresh pumpernickel rye bread completes the feast. The kicker of Thousand Island dressing and full-strength horseradish is available on the side or on the sandwich, and this dish is sure to leave an impression.

WHAT ELSE IS ON THE MENU? Baskets of Burgers with Fries

WHAT'S NEARBY? Recreational Shoal Creek

HOW DO I GET THERE? 6385 Old Hwy. 71; 10 miles south of Joplin off Hwy. 71

HOW TO CONTACT 417-623-8382 | www.undercliff.net

Marthasville-Style Cheesecake

In the Show Me State, we brag about our locally made cheesecake being better than New York–style any day! Judy Gross, proprietor of the CRITTER COTTAGE B&B in Marthasville, has been proving this point statewide in the cheesecake she has made for more than ten years. She serves it to her guests and anyone else who wants to order them.

The four-by-six-inch round cake is made to order topped with your favorite fruit, chocolate chips, gnash, or just plain, which most folks prefer.

Critter Cottage is five miles off Highway 47, so you can take in the deer, wild turkey, and all the beauty the woods have to offer. The cottage is an 1860s two-story log cabin, with rustic décor and furnishings that take you back in time. You will sleep on an antique rope bed and wake up to a full breakfast brought to you in the woods. They never had it this good in 1860!

WHAT ELSE IS ON THE MENU? Dinner can be brought to you as well for an additional charge

WHAT'S NEARBY? Eight wineries, nine restaurants, and the Katy Trail

HOW DO I GET THERE? 505 White Tail Lane; Hwy. 47 to Convention Center Dr. to Whitetail

HOW TO CONTACT 636-433-2711 | www.crittercottagebandb.com

Historic Chili Parlor

Open since 1919, DIXON'S CHILI PARLOR is now the oldest family owned restaurant in the state of Missouri. Located in Independence, home of Harry Truman, it was one of President Truman's favorite restaurants before and after his presidency.

The hottest and most popular dish is the Tamale Spread, a plate of tomatoes covered with a huge layer of chili meat. Now that's unique! The chili can be served many ways, which pleases many customers.

The vintage red and white décor with its formica tables and chrome chairs is just the ticket for a real historic chili parlor. Few spaces are available at the counter, and you yell out your order to the cook!

Terry Smith and her son Steven Steffes ensure chili continues to be the focus of this historic business that caters to chili lovers across the state.

There also is a location in Lee Summit, Missouri.

WHAT ELSE IS ON THE MENU? A Dixon Burger, Which Is Chili
Meat on Toasted Bun

WHAT'S NEARBY? Kauffman Stadium

HOW DO I GET THERE? 9105 E. Hwy. 40; I-70 to 40

HOW TO CONTACT 816-861-7308

Not All About the Pie

The ever-famous Coconut Cream Pie is the signature dish at the MOTHER-IN-LAW HOUSE Restaurant in historic St. Charles. The flakey, thin pie crust with its airy coconut cream was a recipe from an early employee, who did not reveal her secret until she lay on her death bed. She would come to work earlier than everyone else, so no one would know her recipe. She said, "The recipe came with me and would die with me."

Donna Hafer, the owner of the restaurant and recipient of the recipe, greets her guests each evening in the Victorian 1800s building that was constructed to accommodate a mother-in-law. The mother-in-law spirit was not originally kind to Donna, until a psychic told her that Donna needed to make the mother-in-law feel welcome. Donna and her staff began telling the mother-in-law that they loved her each night before they went home, and now all is well.

Donna encourages everyone to try her amazing pie, which she was so fortunate to inherit. Oh, and when you visit, don't forget to tell the mother-in-law that you love her on your way out the door!

WHAT ELSE IS ON THE MENU? Donna's Blend of Poppy Seed Dressing, which you can purchase by the bottle and take home

WHAT'S NEARBY? Missouri's First State Capitol down the street

HOW DO I GET THERE? 500 S. Main St.; I-70 toward the Missouri River to Main St.

HOW TO CONTACT 636-946-9444 | www.motherinlawhouse.com

Soup with the Eagles

THE VILLAGE OF THE BLUE ROSE offers many experiences that represent Missouri at its best! This is a unique restaurant, bed and breakfast, excellent hiking and boating location, and a great eagle-watching spot. You can also hear live bluegrass music from 4 p.m. to 8 p.m. most evenings. Word is this place is the best-kept secret in Pike County.

When it comes to food, Chef Doug Nickels offers many award-winning recipes, and cheese potato soup served with warm, crusty bread is his favorite. Everyone comes back for more.

Dining in this village restaurant offers breathtaking views of the Mississippi River from its glass-lined walls. The Blue Rose also hosts all types of banquets.

The Village is a nonprofit organization employing many people with special needs, many of whom work and live there as well.

WHAT ELSE IS ON THE MENU? Great Chicken Croissant Sandwiches

WHAT'S NEARBY? The Village's Red Barn Shop, which has antiques and gifts

HOW DO I GET THERE? 12533 Hwy. 79; I-70 to Hwy. 79

HOW TO CONTACT 573-242-3539 | www.villagebluerose.org

Fresh as a Missouri Morning

This slogan "fresh as a Missouri Morning" has worked well over the years for the CENTRAL DAIRY in Jefferson City. This longtime institution, owned by the Hackman family, is known throughout the state for its luscious homemade ice cream that comes in thirty different flavors. Besides vanilla, of course, its bestseller is Moose Tracks, an Alaskan classic flavor of vanilla, fudge, and peanut butter. They will be happy to pack you a quart of your favorite flavor to take home with you.

The nostalgic ice cream parlor touts its large banana splits, big enough for the entire family to share and good enough to keep them coming back.

There are very few dairies that make and serve ice cream on the premises, but here more than one hundred employees work in the plant, parlor, or drive the thirty-five routes for ice cream deliveries. At Central Dairy, generations have something wonderful and delicious in common, so you may want to be a part of it. There is a second location in Columbia, Missouri.

WHAT ELSE IS ON THE MENU? Old-Fashioned Hot Dog with a Fountain Cherry Coke

WHAT'S NEARBY? 10 blocks from the Missouri State Capitol

HOW DO I GET THERE? 610 Madison St.; Hwy. 54 to 50 to Madison

HOW TO CONTACT 573-635-6148 | www.centraldairy.biz

The Home of Pan-Fried Chicken

How long has it been since you were served fried chicken right out of an iron skillet, like your mother or grandmother used to make? STROUD'S RESTAURANT, located in a scenic farmhouse setting, takes that a step further in its menu by serving its famous fried chicken family style.

Housed in an original 1829 log cabin that once entertained the Confederates with delicacies cooked over an open fire, the site has become known nationally as one of Kansas City's best restaurants. Besides many awards, Stroud's has received recognition in publications like the *Wall Street Journal, Gourmet Magazine,* and the *New York Times*.

Proprietor Mike Donegan is pleased to carry on the tradition of reminding people that good home cooking does not have to occur at home! Who could not agree with that?

There is a second location in Fairway, Kansas.

WHAT ELSE IS ON THE MENU? Tender Broiled Pork Chops

WHAT'S NEARBY? Athletic and Golf Club of Maple Creek

HOW DO I GET THERE? 5410 N.E. Oak Ridge Rd.; take I-35 exit to 10

HOW TO CONTACT 816-454-9600 | www.stroudsrestaurant.com

Your Thrill on Blueberry Hill

There is more than one thrill at the famous rock and roll restaurant called BLUEBERRY HILL in St. Louis. Just like the era it so nicely represents, the hamburger is the feature on the menu. If you enjoy hamburgers, you will have trouble deciding which of the five varieties to choose from. All are 100 percent ground chuck, with many condiments to choose from. It's no wonder Blueberry Hill has been voted "best hamburger" in St. Louis time and again. If you are a vegetarian, you may want to try the Veggie Burger with eleven ingredients served on a bulgur wheat bun.

Joe and Linda Edwards opened this nostalgic restaurant in 1979, and it is now a St. Louis landmark. Incredible pop culture collections will amaze you, and entertainment is frequent in their many themed rooms such as the Elvis Room, which displays memorabilia of his era. Famous celebrities like Chuck Berry perform regularly. Open seven days a week.

WHAT ELSE IS ON THE MENU? Gazpacho

WHAT'S NEARBY? The St. Louis Walk of Fame and specialty shops

HOW DO I GET THERE? 6504 Delmar Blvd.; I-170 to Delmar east, on the Loop

HOW TO CONTACT 314-727-4444 | www.blueberryhill.com

Barbeque Off a Truck

Charlie Finley's family has been barbequing for more than twenty years. What many locals refer to as "the pit" in Marshall, Missouri, is officially called the BARBEQUE PIT STOP.

Barbeque can be challenging to order, so your best option is to try the Three Meat Dish, which has the meat falling off the bones. It includes ribs, chicken, and beef, and Charlie's favorite sauce will enhance any selection.

This unique eatery is like no other in that it is located in a green and purple house tucked away in a residential neighborhood. For pick-up orders, look for the arrow on the side of the house with "drive thru" painted on it. There is plenty of seating in a nicely decorated interior.

Charlie travels to three other locations in a truck with a barbeque pit on the back, ready to grill. Sedalia and Warrensburg both host this great mobile barbeque, and Roadfood.com has great food photos and praise for this one-of-a-kind Missouri barbeque.

WHAT ELSE IS ON THE MENU? Pulled Pork

WHAT'S NEARBY? Residential neighborhood

HOW DO I GET THERE? 755 West Clay; I-70, Hwy. 65, to West Arrow, S. Miami, West Morgan to Clay

HOW TO CONTACT 660-886-8548

Here's the Juice!

Many publications have rated the GARTH WOODSIDE MAN-SION in Hannibal as the No. 1 bed and breakfast in Missouri, and it has been rated in the top four in the United States by the *Bed and Breakfast Traveler's Magazine.*

This private, gorgeous, Victorian estate owned by John and Julie Roisen offers many unique experiences and memories their guests can take home, but tasting the magic Garth Juice that the owners serve for breakfast each morning is a memory many try to create on their own without success. Is it fruit? Is it a vegetable blend? Or both? The owners also will oblige by cooking something for you from their fruitful garden located on the estate's thirty-nine acres.

It's not all about the juice, however. When you walk the grounds and admire their beauty, you are likely to see three llamas roaming around. Yes, llamas, right here in the Show Me State, waiting to greet their guests. The Dowager House, the Woodside View Cottage, and the Woodside Trail Cottage are also on the property and provide a more secluded setting for those desiring privacy.

WHAT ELSE IS ON THE MENU? Garth Granola for Breakfast
(Recipe on Website)

WHAT'S NEARBY? Four miles to the historic town of Hannibal, home of Mark Twain

HOW DO I GET THERE? 11069 New London Rd.; Hwy. 61, 75 miles north of I-70. Turn right on New London

HOW TO CONTACT 888-427-8409 | www.garthmansion.com

The Home of Toasted Ravioli

St. Louis and Toasted Ravioli are like peanut butter and jelly. When you want to experience the "real deal at the real location," just visit CHARLIE GITTO'S ON THE HILL. Local historians claim toasted ravioli was created in 1947 at a place known as Angelo's, where a chef was transferring ravioli to a pan and it fell into bread crumbs by mistake. He decided to go ahead and fry the breaded pasta, with pleasant results. A dip into great Italian tomato sauce was just the accent it needed, and now the popular combination is known throughout the state. Whether you are enjoying northern or southern cuisine, dining at Charlie Gitto's is the true taste of Italy.

Visiting the historic Hill neighborhood is like visiting "Little Italy." You will find rows of tiny houses, neat lawns, thriving bakeries, grocery stores, and restaurants.

WHAT ELSE IS ON THE MENU? Charlie Gitto's Signature Roasted Shrimp

WHAT'S NEARBY? Historic St. Ambrose Catholic Church

HOW DO I GET THERE? 5226 Shaw Ave.; I-44 to S. Kingshighway, right on Shaw Ave.

HOW TO CONTACT 314-772-8898 | www.charliegittos.com

Custard and Christmas Trees

TED DREWES FROZEN CUSTARD is a St. Louis destination and landmark, and the first location for this frozen custard stand opened on Natural Bridge in 1931. Now the hot spot for visitors far and wide is on Chippewa Street in Southwest St. Louis City, with a second location farther east on Grand Avenue. Many visiting celebrities make sure to stop at Ted Drewes.

The frozen custard is available in twenty-eight different flavors, and the rich custard combinations transition into what is known as a concrete. They have scrumptious names like Hawaiian Delight, Southern Delight, Crater Copernicus, Dutchman Delight, and the ever-popular Terramizzou.

Another attraction that lures customers in the dead of winter, when business at the custard stand is at a standstill, is Ted Drewes Christmas Tree Lot, a favorite spot for picking out that outstanding real Christmas tree. Ted Drewes himself goes to Nova Scotia to select the best Canadian Balsam Fir trees.

Whether you cool off with custard in the summer or select a cool tree for the holidays, pay a visit to Ted Drewes.

WHAT ELSE IS ON THE MENU? Ted Drew Souvenirs

WHAT'S NEARBY? Quaint St. Louis Hills neighborhood

HOW DO I GET THERE? 6726 Chippewa; I-44 to south Hampton to Chippewa

HOW TO CONTACT 314-481-2652 | www.teddrewes.com

A Mansion Breakfast

Imagine waking up in a lavishly restored Victorian bed and breakfast where you are served soufflé pancakes. This delightful breakfast delicacy is from a secret recipe of owner Mary Jo Alter's grandmother, and the pancakes are served with natural maple syrup and fresh fruit. Enjoy breakfast on one of three porches or dine inside the mansion.

This stately 1869 home is known as the RIVERCENE BED AND BREAKFAST, located in New Franklin. Built by riverboat baron Captain Joseph Kinney, the mansion has eleven imported marble fire places, beautiful antiques, three-hundred-pound walnut doors, and a grand staircase whose design the state of Missouri incorporated into its architectural plans for the governor's mansion in Jefferson City.

The famous artist George Caleb Bingham did some of his finest paintings in this home when he stayed here. Unfortunately, he did not get to sample the soufflé pancakes.

WHAT ELSE IS ON THE MENU? Fresh Homemade Bread

WHAT'S NEARBY? The Katy Trail and the Isle of Capri Casino

HOW DO I GET THERE? 127 Country Rd. 463; 3 miles off I-70

HOW TO CONTACT 800-531-0862 | www.rivercene.com

Better Than Witches Brew

The most incredible Baked Potato Soup is concocted daily at THE MAGPIE RESTAURANT in historic St. Charles. Gallons of this popular favorite are made daily because three out of four customers make this menu choice. The rich, thick, creamy delight is loaded with potatoes, cheese, bacon, and green onions. Fantastic salads and desserts, like the special crepes made by owner Rhonda Crane, are perfect complements to the famous specialty.

The seating is packed in the two rooms, but outdoor seasonal seating is available.

This 1821 building was once owned by the Spanish governor of St. Charles. The home passed through many hands, but in more recent history it became known to the locals as "the witch's house" because the family that lived there practiced "white witchcraft" and had a school of Wicca. You will find a sign in the restaurant stating that the "witch is in."

WHAT ELSE IS ON THE MENU? Cream of Asparagus Soup, the owner's favorite

WHAT'S NEARBY? Historic St. Charles Main St. and specialty shops

HOW DO I GET THERE? 903 S. Main St.; 5 streets down from I-70 off Blanchette Bridge

HOW TO CONTACT 636-947-3883

I've Been Eating on the Railroad

A visit to FRITZ'S RAILROAD RESTAURANT in Kansas City, Missouri, is amusing for anyone who loves the world of trains! The 1954 depot diner has patrons place food orders over the phone from their dining booth. Food is then delivered by an electric train called the "skat cat," which runs from the edge of the ceiling to your table. Drinks are delivered by hand. Children under twelve receive a paper railroad hat, and other train memorabilia will keep your eyes occupied as well. Fred Kropf now operates the restaurant, which was founded by his father, Fritz.

The fun hamburger choice is the Gen Dare, a small, single hamburger topped with hash browns, grilled onions, melted cheese, ketchup, mustard, and pickle on a seeded bun. It is crunchy, tasty, and you can't eat just one! Add a shake and onion rings to make your visit to Fritz's filling and fun!

Fritz's drive-through window is another option, and there is a second location at the Crown Plaza Shopping Center.

WHAT ELSE IS ON THE MENU? A Hearty Breakfast Menu

WHAT'S NEARBY? Residential neighborhood

HOW DO I GET THERE? 250 N. 18th St.; I-70 to 18th St. Expressway

HOW TO CONTACT 913-281-2777

Sources

In addition to personal interviews with restaurant owners, employees, and patrons, the following people assisted me with obtaining information about the featured restaurants. They also helped me identify and locate the restaurants that appear in this book.

1. Mary Ann Kemper, Troy
   Joyce@purplequilter.com
2. Anonymous
3. Heather Berry, *Rural Missouri Magazine*
   Michael Hoffman, Branson
4. Jeff Robinson, Kirksville
5. Jessica Homin, West Plains
   Sharon Danning, West Plains
6. Bobbie Kuschel, St. Charles
7. Linda Martin, Mexico
   Linda Sappington, Ashland
   Bobbie Gross, Mexico
8. Thomas Brueles, Warrensburg
9. Ed Johnson, Columbia
   Bettina Havig, Columbia
10. Marlene Crane, Williamsburg
11. Chris Mercier, Kansas City
12. Verna Piecer, Cole Camp
    Diana Pornia, Deep Water
13. Zelda Keith, Memphis
    Jim McCarty, *Rural Missouri Magazine*
14. Claudia Vega, Mexico

Kendra Rogers, Mexico
15. Melissa Matteson, Albany
16. Keith Hazelwood, St. Charles
17. Pam Infranco, Trenton
    Carol Westcott, Trenton
18. Heather Berry, *Rural Missouri Magazine*
19. Peter Hahn, Kansas City
    Hallye Bone, St. Charles
20. Tessa Pruitt, Fulton
    Connie Gresham, Millersburg
21. Anonymous
22. Ann Ramotasky, St. Louis
    Gregory Becker, St. Louis
23. Priscilla Strobe, Columbia
24. Marilyn Kirby, Fayette
    Sandy Stirlwalt, Thomas Hill
25. Steve Elhmann, St. Charles
26. Bud Casey, and Sarah Lee, Moberly
27. Aaron Elliot, St. Louis
    Linda Montgomery, St. Louis
28. Donna Zigler, Lake of the Ozarks
29. Drake Dawson, New Bloomfield

30. Lynda Lorenz, Frohna
31. Bell Grace, St. Joseph
32. Sheila Greenwall, Haiti
33. Judi Gross, Marthasville
34. Lynn Phelps, Greenwood
35. Greg Brockmeier, Columbia
36. Brian Bardo, Lee Summit
    Sara Craig, Harrisonville
37. Bill Grace, St. Joseph
38. Pam Beaver, Joplin,
39. Gary Dyer, Lebanon
    Donna Bricket, Lebanon
40. Donna Marion, Neosho
    Chuck Craig, Neosho
41. Joe Eisenbraun, St. Louis
42. Jessica Hendrickson, Cuba
    Audrey Hahn, Hazelwood
43. Keith Hazelwood, St. Charles
44. Mary Ann Kemper, Troy
45. Laurel Norton, Louisiana
    Mary Ann Kemper, Troy
    Karen Stuckey, Louisiana
46. Amanda Seyer, Cape Girardeau
47. Austin Duree, Springfield
    Bob Haik, Springfield
48. Cathy McGeorge, Fulton
49. Brian Bardo, Lee Summit
50. Gail Long, Branson
51. Josh Stevens, St. Louis
52. Heather Berry, *Rural Missouri Magazine*

Barb Combes, Stockton
Martha Ethridge, Rolla
53. Martha Ethridge, Rolla
54. Amy Person, Lee Summit
55. Barbara Razer, Sikeston
56. Jason Watkins, New York, NY
57. Michelle Standridge, Jackson
58. Joyce Davis, Salem
59. Connie Hughes, Richland
    www.roadsideamerica.com/tip/4102
60. McKalla Stevens, Chi clothe
61. Linda Sappington, Ashland
    Mike Cooper, Columbia
62. Diane Roal, Augusta
    Bill and Chris Shal, Defiance
63. Jamie Inman, St. Genevieve
64. Ed Hutchinson, Kansas City
    2008 Best of Missouri in *Rural Missouri Magazine*
65. Teresa Leimkuler, Morrison
    Linda Nelson, Loose Creek
66. Trent Starks, Point Look Out
67. Myra Oviatt, Miller
    Jerrett Medlin, *Rural Missouri Magazine*
    Ozark, *Missouri Magazine*
68. Steven and Linda Simon, Fredericksburg
69. Heather Berry, *Rural Missouri Magazine*
    Ruth Noblett, Stockton

70. Belinda Harrrison, Springfield
71. Bill Massa, Kirkwood
    Tony and Vicki Petzoldt, Kirkwood
72. Hazel Bacon, Kansas City
    Madeline Matson, *Foods of Missouri*, page 72
73. Lisa Perry, California
    Sandra Ratcliff, California
    Madeline Matson, *Foods of Missouri*
74. Reba Starling, Silvey
75. Anonymous
76. Heather Berry, *Rural Missouri Magazine*
77. Kim Warner, Kimmswick
78. Tim Keller, Lake St. Louis
    Ree Chapman, Lake St. Louis
79. Angie Hackele, Perryville
80. Courtney Winnie Weber, Eminence
81. Paul and Debbie Bisges, Jefferson City
82. Lure Restaurant Reviews www.ozarksmag.com

83. Chris and Bill Shal, Defiance
    Kate Filla, Washington
84. Donna Baker, Fayette
85. Marilyn Kempfer, Glen Carbon
86. Melissa Winn, Joplin
87. Judy Gross, Marthasville
88. Beth Green, Bella's Online
    Steven Stresses, Independence
89. Donna and Bob Hafer, St. Charles
90. Doug Nickles, Clarksville
91. Robert Schultz, Jefferson City
    Christopher Hackman, Jefferson City
    www.judybrook.com
92. Anonymous
93. Robert Hazelwood, St. Louis
94. Betty Lenz, Marshal
95. Julie Rolsen, Hannibal
96. Anonymous
97. Anonymous
98. Mary Jo Alter, New Franklin
99. Rhonda ------
100. Chris Eastman, Kansas City

Locations
by Region

Kansas City

8 Warrensburg (Monetti's)

11 Kansas City (Classic Cup Café)

12 Lincoln (Charley's Buffet)

15 Albany (Poppa's Restaurant)

16 Kansas City (Piropos)

17 Trenton (Wild Onion Flowers and Café)

19 Kansas City (Raphael)

21 Sedalia (Kehde's Barbeque)

31 St. Joseph (Barbosa's Castillo)

34 Greenwood (Perazelli's)

36 Harrisonville (Pearl Street Grill)

37 St. Joseph (Galvin's)

54 Sikeston (Marina Grog)

60 Chillicothe (Wabash Barbeque)

72 Kansas City (Bryant's Barbeque)

76 Greenville (Tupelo Honey's)

88 Independence (Dixon's)

92 Independence (Stroud's)

94 Marshall (Barbeque Pit Stop)

100 Kansas City (Fritz's Railroad)

Springfield

Macon

St. Louis

1 Troy (Krumbly Burger)

2 St. Charles (Premiere Café)

22 St. Louis (Boathouse)

27 St. Louis (Sweetie Pies)

33 Labadie (3 Brothers)

41 St. Louis (Crown Candy)

43 O'Fallon (McGurk's)

44 Elsberry (4th Street)

51 St. Louis (Goody Goody Diner)

55 Sikeston (Lambert's Café)

56 St. Charles (Pio's)

62 Defiance (Wine Country Garden)

71 Kirkwood (Massa's)

75 Hermann (Wurstfest)

77 Kimmswick (Blue Owl)

78 Dardenne Prairie (Louisiana)

83 Washington (American Bounty)

87 Marthasville (Critter Cottage)

89 St. Charles (Mother-in-Law)

93 St. Louis (Blueberry Hill)

96 St. Louis (Charlie Gitto's)

97 St. Louis (Ted Drewes)

99 St. Charles (Magpie)

Poplar Bluff

5 West Plains (Cup O' Joe)

30 Frohna (Saxon Memorial)

32 Hayti (Chubby's Barbeque)

42 Cuba (Missouri Hicks Barbeque)

46 Cape Girardeau (Royal N'Orleans)

52 St. James (Sybil's St. James)

57 Jackson (Lil' Miss Muffins)

58 Salem (Main Street Café)

63 Ste. Genevieve (Hotel Ste. Genevieve)

79 Perryville (Hoeckele Bakery)

80 Eminence (Winfield's)

85 Perryville (Ewald's)

Index

About the Author

Ann Hazelwood is a Missouri native, born in Perryville. Her adult life brought her to Historic St. Charles, where she restored a historic home and raised her two sons, Joel and Jason.

In 1979, she opened Patches etc. on the street where she lived. As her career developed, she became a Certified Quilt Appraiser, which takes her around the country for lectures and services. She is also a recognized quilt book author for the American Quilting Society of Paducah, Kentucky.

In 2009, Ann sold her business to another owner to be able to spend more time writing. This encouraged her to write *100 Things To Do In and Around St. Charles,* followed by *100 Best Kept Secrets of Missouri.*

100 Unique Eats and Eateries in Missouri was a natural sequence of interest to her other books. The focus was to find an eatery that was known for a particular food item, followed by other unique experiences.

Ann's love of her home state has inspired her to lecture on *Missouri Travel.* She feels Missouri has offered her a wonderful quality of life, and she wants to share it with you.